Cambridge En Proficiency Practice Tests

Five tests for Cambridge English: Proficiency

MARK HARRISON

OXFORD
UNIVERSITY PRESS

OXFORD
UNIVERSITY PRESS

Great Clarendon Street, Oxford, OX2 6DP, United Kingdom

Oxford University Press is a department of the University of Oxford.
It furthers the University's objective of excellence in research, scholarship,
and education by publishing worldwide. Oxford is a registered trade
mark of Oxford University Press in the UK and in certain other countries

© Oxford University Press 2012

The moral rights of the author have been asserted

First published in 2012

2020

12

Photocopying

The Publisher grants permission for the photocopying of those pages marked
'photocopiable' according to the following conditions. Individual purchasers
may make copies for their own use or for use by classes that they teach.
School purchasers may make copies for use by staff and students, but this
permission does not extend to additional schools or branches

Under no circumstances may any part of this book be photocopied for resale

ISBN: 978 0 19 457735 9

Printed in China

This book is printed on paper from certified and well-managed sources

ACKNOWLEDGEMENTS

*The authors and publisher are grateful to those who have given permission to reproduce
the following extracts and adaptations of copyright material:* p.8 Extract from 'Charles
Schulz: Obituary', *The Daily Telegraph*, 14 February 2000. © Telegraph Media
Group Limited 2000; p.9 Extract from 'Behind the scenes' by Matthew Nixson,
The Times, 6 November 1997. Reproduced by permission of NI Syndication;
p.12 Extract from *Soft City* by Jonathan Raban. Copyright © Jonathan Raban,
1974. Reproduced by permission of Pan Macmillan, London and Aitken
Alexander Associates Limited; p.17 Extract from 'Cooking with Chocolate: The
last word on chocolate', *The Telegraph*, 21 October 2011. © Telegraph Media
Group Limited 2011; p.14 Extract from *Streets Ahead* by Keith Waterhouse
published by Hodder & Stoughton. Reproduced by permission of David
Higham Associates; p.18 Extract from Pgs xix and 27 of *The Green Travel Guide*
by Greg Neale. © 1998. Reproduced by permission of Taylor & Francis Books
(UK); p.20 Extract from 'The clash of the two cultures' by Graham Farmelo,
The Daily Telegraph, 10 March 1999. © Telegraph Media Group Limited 1999;
p.20 Extract from 'As others see us: The flight booker' by Susan d'Arcy, *The
Sunday Times*, 6 April 1997. Reproduced by permission of NI Syndication;
p.22 Extract from *In the Psychiatrist's Chair* by Anthony Clare. Reproduced by
permission of The Random House Group Limited, and A P Watt Ltd on behalf
of Professor Anthony Clare; p.28 Extract from 'A curse on this cult of celebrity'
by Ray Connolly, *The Daily Mail*, 25 February 2000. Reproduced by permission
of Solo Syndication; p.32 Extract from *Solomon Grundy* by Dan Gooch. Reproduced
with permission of Curtis Brown Group Lts, London on behalf of Dan Gooch.
© Dan Gooch, 1997; p.34 Extract from *Staying Up* by Rick Gekoski. Copyright
© Rick Gekoski 1998. Reproduced by permission of the author c/o Rogers,
Coleridge & White Ltd., 20 Powis Mews, London W11 1JN, and Little Brown
Book Group; p.37 Extract from 'Could a treadmill desk save your life?' by John
Preston, *The Telegraph*, 4 December 2011. © Telegraph Media Group Limited 2011;
p.38 Extract from *The Language of Clothes* by Alison Lurie. Copyright © 1981, 2000
by Alison Lurie. Reprinted by permission of Melanie Jackson Agency, L.L.C,
and A P Watt Ltd Literary Agents; p.41 Extract from 'My sporting passion-
scuba diving' by Emily Hohler, *The Sunday Telegraph*, 5 May 1996. © Telegraph
Media Group Limited 1996; p.42 Extract from *Winning Consumer Competitions* by
Kathy Kantypowicz, published by How to Books Ltd. Reproduced by permission;
p.47 Extract from *Birdsong* by Sebastian Faulks, copyright © 1993 by Sebastian
Faulks. Used by permission of Random House, Inc. and The Random House
Group Limited; p.48 Extract from 'On the island where dreams came true' by
Janet Daley, *The Daily Telegraph*, 27 December 1999. © Telegraph Media Group
Limited 1999; p.49 Extract from 'You can't judge an author by his cover' by

Charles Lawrence, *The Daily Telegraph*, 5 December 1996. © Telegraph Media
Group Limited 1996; p.52 Extract from *Morecambe & Wise* by Graham McCann.
© Graham McCann 1998. Reprinted by permission of HarperCollins Publishers
Ltd and Mic Cheetham Literary Agency; p.54 Extract from *Dead Souls* by Ian
Rankin. © John Rebus Ltd 1999, Orion, an imprint of The Orion Publishing
Group, London. Reproduced by permission; p.57 Extract from 'Shining lights:
the new independent jewellery designers' by Sophie de Rosee, *The Daily Telegraph*,
17 December 2011. © Telegraph Media Group Limited 2011; p.58 Extract from
Children's Games in Street and Playground by Iona and Peter Opie (1984). By
permission of Oxford University Press; p.58 Extract from *Children's Games with
Things* by Iona and Peter Opie (1997). By permission of Oxford University Press;
p.60 Extract from 'Learning on a critical job' by Laura Merrill, *The Daily Telegraph*,
29 May 1999. © Telegraph Media Group Limited 1999; p.60 Extract from *Big
Mouth Strikes Again* by Tony Parsons. Reproduced by permission of Tony Parsons;
p.61 Extract from 'Home is where the art is' by Oliver Bennett, *The Times*,
15 March 1997. Reproduced by permission of NI Syndication; p.62 Extract
from *Football Man* by Arthur Hopcraft. Reproduced by permission of Aurum
Press; p.67 Extract from 'The roar of the greenbacks' by Nigel Cliff, *The Times*,
2 July 1998. Reproduced by permission of NI Syndication; p.68 Extract from
'Karaoke culture rules OK?' by Rory Bremner, *The Daily Telegraph*, 25 September
1998. © Telegraph Media Group Limited 1998; p.72 Extract from *Lily White* by
Susan Isaacs. Copyright (c) 1996 by Susan Isaacs. Reproduced by permission of
HarperCollins Publishers, and Susan Isaacs; p.74 Extract from 'Help guide us
through the universe' by Sir Martin Rees, *The Daily Telegraph*, 2 December 1998.
© Telegraph Media Group Limited 1998; p.77 Extract from 'Desperately seeking
wise old Socrates' by Bettany Hughes, *The Telegraph*, 12 October 2010. © Telegraph
Media Group Limited 2010; p.78 Extract from The Introduction from *Ideas of
Human Nature* by Roger Trigg, John Wiley & Sons Ltd. Reproduced by permission;
p.80 Extract from 'A place for damsels in distress' by Bill Powell, *Daily Telegraph*,
21 August 1999. © Telegraph Media Group Limited 1999; p.80 Extract from
'Meet the million-dollar toy boy' by Charles Laurence, *The Daily Telegraph*,
29 April 1999. © Telegraph Media Group Limited 1999; p.80 Extract from
'Cookbooks: love affairs with no calories' by Nigella Lawson, *The Daily Telegraph*,
26 September 1998. © Telegraph Media Group Limited 1998; p.81 Extract from
'Persuading us to Shop Till We Drop' by Charles Clover, *The Daily Telegraph*,
2 January 1999. © Telegraph Media Group Limited 1999; p.82 Extract from
Hunting People by Hunter Davies, Mainstream Publishing Co. (Edinburgh) Ltd.
Reproduced by permission.

*Although every effort has been made to trace and contact copyright holders before
publication, this has not been possible in some cases. We apologize for any apparent
infringement of copyright and if notified, the publisher will be pleased to rectify any
errors or omissions at the earliest opportunity.*

Source: p.38 Extract from *Understanding Fashion* by Elizabeth Rouse, John Wiley
& Sons Ltd.

*The publisher would also like to thank the following for permission to reproduce
photographs:* Alamy Images pp.44 (Young male using computer/aberCPC), 64 (man sat on
sofa/Paul Ridsdale), 84 (1960's Lancia/Goddard Automotive), 84 (P&O Oceana/
Greg Balfour Evans), 84 (Hitchhiking in Bosnia/Jason Langley), 84 (easy jet/Nick
Hanna); Corbis pp.24 (UK – Students March Against Tuition Fees/Mike Kemp),
24 (Politician shaking hands with supporters/Hill Street Studios), 84 (Commuters
on Tokyo Subway Car/Paul Souders); Getty Images pp.24 (Two students talking/
IMAGEMORE Co), 44 (watching television/Family in living room), 44 (Man with
burning money and cigar/Jupiterimages), 44 (Wimbledon/Michael Regan);
Oxford University Press p.44 (Celebrity Couple/Moodboard RF); Rex Features
p.24 (American football/Eye Candy).

Pages 87–93 reproduced with permission of Cambridge ESOL.

Sample answer Test 1 Question 1 written by Dominika Gajek.

Contents

Introduction

This book contains:

- Four complete Practice Tests for Cambridge English: Proficiency (from March 2013)
- Explanatory Key
  This provides detailed explanations for correct answers, and also for incorrect answers in Reading and Use of English Part 1. Relevant vocabulary and grammatical points are also fully explained.
- Sample answers for the Writing Paper
  There is a sample student answer for each of the kinds of writing required (essay, article, letter, etc.) and all the sample answers are assessed.
- General assessment criteria for Writing and Speaking Papers
- Sample answer sheets
- Audio scripts

There are four Papers in the exam:

Reading and Use of English (1 hour 30 minutes)

	Text	Question type	Focus
PART 1	1 short text with 8 gaps	Multiple-choice cloze 4-option multiple-choice; choose the correct word(s) to fill each gap	vocabulary (meaning of single words, completion of phrases, phrasal verbs, etc.) **8 questions; 8 marks**
PART 2	1 short text with 8 gaps	Open cloze fill each gap with one word	mostly grammar, some vocabulary **8 questions; 8 marks**
PART 3	1 short text with 8 gaps	Word formation use the words given to form the correct word for each gap	vocabulary **8 questions; 8 marks**
PART 4	6 unrelated sentences, each followed by a single word and a gapped sentence	Key word transformations use the word given to complete the gapped sentence so that it means the same as the first sentence	grammar, vocabulary and collocation **6 questions; 12 marks** (1 mark for each part of the answer, max. 2 marks per question)
PART 5	1 long text	Multiple choice 4-option multiple choice	comprehension of detail, opinion, attitude, tone, purpose, main idea, implication, exemplification, reference, etc. **6 questions; 12 marks**
PART 6	1 text with 7 paragraphs missing	Gapped text choice of 8 paragraphs to fill the gaps	understanding of text structure, links between parts of text **7 questions; 14 marks**
PART 7	1 text divided into sections OR several short texts	Multiple matching matching statements / information to section of text or short text they refer to or appear in	detail, opinion, attitude, specific information **10 questions; 10 marks**

Writing (1 hour 30 minutes)

Each question carries equal marks.

	Task	Word limit
PART 1	essay summarizing the key points in two short texts and giving opinions Candidates **must** do this task.	240–280 words
PART 2	article, report, review, letter Questions 2–4: candidates choose one task from three choices OR Questions 5a / 5b: candidates may choose one task about the set books. (There are two set books which change periodically)	280–320 words

Listening (40 minutes)

Each question carries equal marks.

	Task	Question type	Focus
PART 1	3 short unrelated pieces (monologue or conversation)	Multiple choice 3-option multiple-choice (2 questions per piece)	detail, gist, opinion, feeling, attitude, purpose, agreement between speakers, course of action **6 questions; 6 marks**
PART 2	1 monologue	Sentence completion 9 sentences to complete with a word or short phrase	understanding of specific information given in the piece **9 questions; 9 marks**
PART 3	1 interview or discussion (two or more speakers)	Multiple choice 4-option multiple-choice	understanding of opinion, attitude, detail, gist, inference **5 questions; 5 marks**
PART 4	5 short themed monologues	Multiple matching 2 tasks. For each task, match what each speaker says to one of 8 options	same as Part 1 **10 questions; 10 marks**

Speaking (14 minutes)

	Activity type (examiner + two candidates)	Focus
PART 1	conversation between candidates and examiner (2 mins)	general and personal topics relating to the candidate
PART 2	talking about pictures: candidates discuss together one or more pictures and do a decision-making task (4 minutes)	exchanging ideas, giving and justifying opinions, making suggestions, agreeing/disagreeing, reaching a decision through negotiation
PART 3	each candidate speaks alone for 2 minutes, based on a prompt card; each candidate is also asked a question about what the other candidate said discussion between candidates and examiner on the same topics (10 minutes)	speaking continuously on a given topic, commenting on what someone has said exchanging ideas, giving and justifying opinions, agreeing/disagreeing

READING & USE OF ENGLISH   1 hour 30 minutes

PART 1

*For questions 1–8, read the text below and decide which answer (A, B, C or D) best fits each gap. Mark your answers **on the separate answer sheet**.*

There is an example at the beginning (0).

Example:

0   A acclaiming   **B** plugging   **C** raving   **D** promoting

0	A	B	C	D

Reading People

Last month I was invited to lunch with my cousin and his new wife. I hadn't met her before, but my cousin had been **0** *C* to everyone about her wonderful, warm and caring personality. Clearly she had completely **1**_____ him off his feet. It didn't take long for me to see through this veneer. On arriving at lunch, she sat down at the table without so **2**_____ as an acknowledgment of my presence. She **3**_____ to continue her conversation with her husband as if I didn't exist, and then **4**_____ at the young waitress for accidentally spilling some water on the table. I was eventually **5**_____ worthy of her attention only when it came to paying the bill; I had offered to treat them to lunch to celebrate their recent 'good news'. She was evidently someone who could turn the charm on, but only when it **6**_____ her purpose. In my opinion, **7**_____ wonderful, warm and caring people do not blow hot and cold in their behaviour to others **8**_____ on what they believe they can get out of them.of what someone can do for them.

1	**A** plucked	**B** swept	**C** dragged	**D** hoisted
2	**A** much	**B** far	**C** great	**D** long
3	**A** proceeded	**B** followed	**C** progressed	**D** continued
4	**A** winked	**B** glared	**C** peeped	**D** eyed
5	**A** pondered	**B** discriminated	**C** weighed	**D** deemed
6	**A** met	**B** realized	**C** performed	**D** served
7	**A** fully	**B** purely	**C** literally	**D** truly
8	**A** varying	**B** revolving	**C** depending	**D** determined

PART 2

For questions 9–16, read the text below and think of the word which best fits each gap. Use only one word in each gap. There is an example at the beginning (0). Write your answers IN CAPITAL LETTERS on the separate answer sheet.

Example:

0	O	T	H	E	R								

Charles Schulz

The cartoonist Charles Schulz created the daily lives of Charlie Brown, Snoopy, Lucy and the **0** _other_ inhabitants of the *Peanuts* strip. Schulz, **9**_____ to his friends as 'Sparky', drew the daily strip for almost 50 years. Its distinctly American culture **10**_____ nothing to hamper its universal success. It was said to have 355 million readers in 75 countries, and it **11**_____ Schulz very rich. Schulz displayed unflaggingly sharp observation and a fairly gentle, if sometimes downbeat, humour.

He was given **12**_____ anxiety and low spirits, and there was an underlying sadness in his stories, a bitter-sweet quality that clearly fascinated many of his fans. In the 1950s, the strip had a vogue following **13**_____ intellectuals, but Schulz was happy to point **14**_____ that he himself had flunked algebra, Latin, English and physics at school. When someone **15**_____ him an existentialist, he had to ask **16**_____ the word meant.

For questions **17–24**, read the text below. Use the word given in capitals at the end of some of the lines to form a word that fits in the gap in the same line. There is an example at the beginning (**0**). Write your answers **IN CAPITAL LETTERS on the separate answer sheet.**

Example:

| 0 | E | F | F | O | R | T | L | E | S | S | | | |

TEST 1

BEHIND THE SCENES

Watching a successful theatre production is an amazing experience.

The performance looks **0** _effortless_ and everything goes smoothly   **EFFORT**

but this often **17**_____ the amount of work that was actually involved.   **LIE**

At the Palace Theatre, the average time from the first **18**_____ to   **REHEARSE**

opening night is just four weeks of intensive work. Everyone involved attends

the first read-through by the cast, so this is an ideal opportunity to get an

19_____ into how a production germinates.   **SIGHT**

I took myself to the theatre on a **20**_____ October morning to attend the   **CHILL**

read-through of the theatre's new production – the British première of *Sive*, by

the acclaimed Irish playwright John B Keane. It is a poignant portrayal of rural

family life, rich in comedy and filled with **21**_____ characters played   **MEMORY**

by an Irish cast for linguistic **22**_____ .   **AUTHENTIC**

'It's important for people to have a sense of common purpose and

23_____ ,' explains director Ben Barnes. 'The play has been in   **TEAM**

pre-production since June but this is the first reading and it will be

24_____ of how the actors work together. And it's for the theatre   **INDICATE**

staff as much as the actors.'

PART 4

*For questions 25–30, complete the second sentence so that it has a similar meaning to the first sentence, using the word given. **Do not change the word given.** You must use between **three** and **eight** words, including the word given. Here is an example (0):*

Example:

0   Dan definitely won't be able to afford a holiday this year.

possiblity

There _____ to afford a holiday this year.

0	is no possibility of Dan being able

*Write **only the missing words** on the separate answer sheet.*

---

25 John has hinted that he doesn't wish to remain in the group any longer.

hint

John has _____ wishes to remain in the group.

26 Five actors were competing for the leading role in the play.

contention

There _____ the leading role in the play.

27 She was concentrating so hard on her work that she didn't notice when I came in.

wrapped

She was _____ that she didn't notice when I came in.

28 They still haven't found out what caused the accident.

cause

They have yet _____ the accident was.

29 I reluctantly signed the contract.

signature

It was with _____ on the contract.

30 Suzanne is far superior to me in terms of technical knowledge.

match

When it comes _____ for Suzanne.

PART 5

You are going to read an extract from a book about life in cities. For questions **31–36**, choose the answer (**A**, **B**, **C** or **D**) which you think fits best according to the text. Mark your answers **on the separate answer sheet.**

Image and the city

In the city, we are barraged with images of the people we might become. Identity is presented as plastic, a matter of possessions and appearances; and a very large proportion of the urban landscape is taken up by slogans, advertisements, flatly photographed images of folk heroes – the man who turned into a sophisticated dandy overnight by drinking a particular brand of drink, the girl who transformed herself into a femme fatale with a squirt of cheap scent. The tone of the wording of these advertisements is usually pert and facetious, comically drowning in its own hyperbole. But the pictures are brutally exact: they reproduce every detail of a style of life, down to the brand of cigarette-lighter, the stone in the ring, and the economic row of books on the shelf.

Yet, if one studies a line of ads across from where one is sitting on a tube train, these images radically conflict with each other. Swap the details about between the pictures, and they are instantly made illegible. If the characters they represent really are heroes, then they clearly have no individual claim to speak for society as a whole. The clean-cut and the shaggy, rakes, innocents, brutes, home-lovers, adventurers, clowns all compete for our attention and invite emulation. As a gallery, they do provide a glossy mirror of the aspirations of a representative city crowd; but it is exceedingly hard to discern a single dominant style, an image of how most people would like to see themselves.

Even in the business of the mass-production of images of identity, this shift from the general to the diverse and particular is quite recent. Consider another line of stills: the back-lit, soft-focus portraits of the first and second generations of great movie stars. There is a degree of romantic unparticularity in the face of each one, as if they were communal dream-projections of society at large. Only in the specialised genres of westerns, farces and gangster movies were stars allowed to have odd, knobbly cadaverous faces. The hero as loner belonged to history or the underworld: he spoke from the perimeter of society, reminding us of its dangerous edges.

The stars of the last decade have looked quite different. Soft-focus photography has gone, to be replaced by a style which searches out warts and bumps, emphasises the uniqueness not the generality of the face. Voices, too, are strenuously idiosyncratic; whines, stammers and low rumbles are exploited as features of 'star quality'. Instead of romantic heroes and heroines, we have a brutalist, hard-edged style in which isolation and egotism are assumed as natural social conditions.

In the movies, as in the city, the sense of stable hierarchy has become increasingly exhausted; we no longer live in a world where we can all share the same values, the same heroes. (It is doubtful whether this world, so beloved of nostalgia moralists, ever existed; but lip-service was paid to it, the pretence, at least, was kept up.) The isolate and the eccentric push towards the centre of the stage; their fashions and mannerisms are presented as having as good a claim to the limelight and the future as those of anyone else. In the crowd on the underground platform, one may observe a honeycomb of fully-worked-out worlds, each private, exclusive, bearing little comparison with its nearest neighbour. What is prized in one is despised in another. There are no clear rules about how one is supposed to manage one's body, dress, talk, or think. Though there are elaborate protocols and etiquettes among particular cults and groups within the city, they subscribe to no common standard.

For the new arrival, this disordered abundance is the city's most evident and alarming quality. He feels as if he has parachuted into a funfair of contradictory imperatives. There are so many people he might become, and a suit of clothes, a make of car, a brand of cigarettes, will go some way towards turning him into a personage even before he has discovered who that personage is. Personal identity has always been deeply rooted in property, but hitherto the relationship has been a simple one – a question of buying what you could afford, and leaving your wealth to announce your status. In the modern city, there are so many things to buy, such a quantity of different kinds of status, that the choice and its attendant anxieties have created a new pornography of taste.

31 What does the writer say about advertisements in the first paragraph?

    A   Certain kinds are considered more effective in cities than others.

    B   The way in which some of them are worded is cleverer than it might appear.

    C   They often depict people that most other people would not care to be like.

    D   The pictures in them accurately reflect the way that some people really live.

32 The writer says that if you look at a line of advertisements on a tube train, it is clear that

    A   city dwellers have very diverse ideas about what image they would like to have.

    B   some images in advertisements have a general appeal that others lack.

    C   city dwellers are more influenced by images on advertisements than other people are.

    D   some images are intended to be representative of everyone's aspirations.

33 What does the writer imply about portraits of old movie stars?

    A   They tried to disguise the less attractive features of their subjects.

    B   Most people did not think they were accurate representations of the stars in them.

    C   They made people feel that their own faces were rather unattractive.

    D   They reflected an era in which people felt basically safe.

34 What does the writer suggest about the stars of the last decade?

    A   Some of them may be uncomfortable about the way they come across.

    B   They make an effort to speak in a way that may not be pleasant on the ear.

    C   They make people wonder whether they should become more selfish.

    D   Most people accept that they are not typical of society as a whole.

35 The writer uses the crowd on an underground platform to exemplify his belief that

    A   no single attitude to life is more common than another in a city.

    B   no one in a city has strict attitudes towards the behaviour of others.

    C   views of what society was like in the past are often inaccurate.

    D   people in cities would like to have more in common with each other.

36 The writer implies that new arrivals in a city may

    A   change the image they wish to have too frequently.

    B   underestimate the importance of wealth.

    C   acquire a certain image without understanding what that involves.

    D   decide that status is of little importance.

PART 6

You are going to read an extract from an autobiography. Seven paragraphs have been removed from the extract. Choose from the paragraphs A–H the one which fits each gap (37–43). There is one extra paragraph which you do not need to use. Mark your answers on the separate answer sheet.

Eilbeck the features editor

I quickly got the hang of working at the *Mirror*. Every morning at eleven we would be expected to cram into Eilbeck's little office for a features conference, when we either had to come up with ideas of our own or suffer ideas to be thrust upon us. Some of Eilbeck's own offerings were bizarre to say the least, but he did get results. I had got an inkling of his creative thinking during my initial interview when he had invited me to match his scrawled impromptu headline with a feature.

37

Some of these brainstorms came off the day's news, some off the wall. About half the ideas worked, a few of them spectacularly. Following a spate of shootings, Eilbeck scrawled 'THIS GUN FOR SALE' on his pad, together with a rough sketch of a revolver. Within hours a writer was back in the office with a handgun and a dramatic piece on the ease with which (he did not mention the little help he had had from the crime staff) he had bought it in Trafalgar Square.

38

Mercifully, none of Eilbeck's extemporised headlines winged their way to me – at least not yet. The pitifully small paper was grossly overstaffed, with half a dozen highly experienced feature writers fighting to fill one page a day, and it was evident that my role was as standby or first reserve. Hanging around the office, where the time was passed pleasantly in chit-chat, smoking and drinking coffee, I was occasionally tossed some small task.

39

Another of my little chores was to compose 'come-ons' for the readers' letters columns – invented, controversial letters that, in a slow week for correspondence, would draw a furious mailbag. I was also put to work rewriting agency and

syndication material that came into the office, including, on occasion, the Sagittarius segment of the astrology column.

40

Some years later, when he had directed his talents to another paper, I confessed to him one day that I had been guilty of tampering in this way. He was in no way put out. It was serenely obvious to him that I had been planted on the *Mirror* by destiny to adjust the hitherto inaccurate information.

41

For example, one afternoon I was summoned to Eilbeck's office to find him in a state of manic excitement, bent over a make-up pad on which he had scrawled 'THE SPICE OF LIFE!' surrounded by a border of stars. This, I was told, was to be the *Mirror's* new three-times-a-week gossip column, starting tomorrow – and I was to be in charge of it.

42

Happily the delightful Eve Chapman was deputed to hold my hand in this insane exercise. The bad news was that Eve, who went home nightly to her parents in Croydon, had never set foot in such a place in her life. We were reduced to raiding the society pages of the glossy magazines and ploughing through *Who's Who* in hopes of finding some important personage with an unusual hobby which could be fleshed out to the maximum twenty-five words.

43

The Spice of Life column itself ground to a halt after our supply of eminent people's interesting pastimes petered out.

A As a result, he wanted no item to be more than twenty-five words long, followed by three dots. He was, at the time, heavily under the influence of Walter Winchell, Earl Wilson and suchlike night-owl columnists in the New York tabloids that were air-freighted to him weekly.

B Flattering though it was to be entrusted with this commission, there was a snag. It had to 'sizzle' – a favourite Eilbeck word – with exclusive snippets about 'the people who really mattered' – to Eilbeck's mind, anyone with an aristocratic title, or money to throw about in casinos and nightclubs. Unfortunately, I did not have a single suitable contact in the whole of London.

C This might be a review copy of some ghosted showbiz memoirs that might be good for a 150-word anecdotal filler. One day Eilbeck dropped a re-issued volume on my desk – *To Beg I am Ashamed*, the supposed autobiography of a criminal. It came complete with one of his headlines: 'IT'S STILL A BAD, DANGEROUS BOOK'. I asked him what was so bad and dangerous about it. 'I haven't read it,' the Features Editor confessed cheerfully. 'Two hundred words by four o'clock'.

D On one desperate occasion, with the deadline looming yet again, we fell to working our way along Millionaires' Row in Kensington, questioning maids and chauffeurs about the foibles of their rich employers. This enterprise came to a stop after someone called the police.

E This proved to be a foretaste of his favourite method of floating an idea. While the assembled feature writers clustered around his desk skimming the newspapers and intermittently quoting some story that might with luck yield a feature angle, Eilbeck would be scribbling away on his pad. Cockily trumpeting his newly minted headline – 'WOULD YOU RISK A BLIND DATE HOLIDAY?' or 'CAN WOMEN BE TRUSTED WITH MONEY?' – he would rip off the page and thrust it into the arms of the nearest writer – 'Copy by four o'clock.'

F This was for the benefit of one of the paper's more irascible executives who was a passionate believer in it. It had been noticed that when he was told he would have a bad day he would react accordingly and his miserable colleagues would go through the day quaking in their shoes. My job was to doctor the entry to give his colleagues a more peaceful ride.

G My month's trial with the *Mirror* quickly expired without my having done anything to justify my existence on the paper, but since Eilbeck didn't mention that my time was up, neither did I. I pottered on, still trying to find my feet. Occasionally opportunity would knock, but it was usually a false alarm. Not always, though.

H But many of Eilbeck's madder flights of fancy had no chance of panning out so well – even I could tell that. Seasoned writers would accept the assignment without demur, repair to a café for a couple of hours, and then ring in to announce that they couldn't make the idea stand up.

PART 7

You are going to read an article about a company that makes chocolate.
For questions 44–53, choose from the sections (A–D). The sections may be
chosen more than once. Mark your answers on the separate answer sheet.

In which section are the following mentioned?

visible evidence of Valrhona's popularity	**44**
assumptions that are not necessarily correct	**45**
the influence of Valrhona on cooking with chocolate	**46**
the difficulty of doing what Valrhona suggests	**47**
a contrast between ways of making chocolate	**48**
a change that Valrhona regretted making	**49**
an explanation of the term used for a stage in a process	**50**
a calculation connected with one of the senses	**51**
the possibility of overdoing something	**52**
an influence on the quality of an ingredient	**53**

The Chocolate Factory

A The scent of chocolate hangs over the small French town of Tain-l'Hermitage. Wafting from savoury to toasted, fruity to oily, the aroma emanates from the 89-year-old factory of Valrhona, one of the most respected chocolate makers in the business. I was inhaling this heady perfume on a trip to find out about Valrhona's first book, the fabulous *Cooking with Chocolate*. A vast tome, it's a chocophile's dream, with pages of chocolate information alongside recipes, from the ultimate sachertorte to 'Bittersweet Chocolate Bars, Salted Butter Caramel and Crystallised Almonds'. Most are mesmerizingly complex creations strictly for trained chefs or time-rich amateurs; mouthwatering for the rest of us. Best of all are the pages on techniques such as the all-important tempering (a heating and cooling process that keeps the shine and texture of chocolate when it is remoulded), all minutely described and carefully illustrated.

B I'd expect nothing less from Valrhona, which we have to thank for the quiet revolution in chocolate of the past 25 years. Back in the early 1980s, plain chocolate meant a cocoa solids content of barely 40 per cent. Then, in the early 1990s, cookery writers began telling us to use chocolate with 'minimum 50 per cent cocoa solids'. The supermarkets started stocking real cooking chocolate with escalating levels of cocoa solids. It was Valrhona that first introduced a 70 per cent cocoa solids chocolate bar to the market in 1986. It caused a flurry among chefs, who found that it gave a far more intense chocolate flavour to their dishes, and it was given star billing on menus. Since then an army of boutique chocolate makers has been born. They all produce chocolate in a 'bean-to-bar' process, transforming raw, fermented beans into chocolate themselves. It's an important distinction, as many other companies buy ready-made chocolate in bulk and re-melt it to form bars and chocolate sweets.

C Inside Valrhona's newest factory on the outskirts of town, Luce, our elegantly grey-haired guide, leads us past paintings of the chefs who are fans of Valrhona. The smell grows ever headier and sweeter as we enter a windowless, high-ceilinged room with a cream-tiled floor, on which neat rows of sacks are waiting for processing. Inside are fermented and dried beans, but the dull brown seeds have a long way to go before they can live up to their botanical name, Theobroma: 'food of the gods'. In the next room that process is beginning, as the beans are roasted in huge rotating drums, then cooled and crushed to peppercorn-sized pieces. Just across the room, a lone worker is supervising the grinding of the nibs through pairs of rollers. It's this powder, he explains, which constitutes the 'cocoa solids' in the chocolate bar, and is mixed with extra cocoa butter (the fatty component of the cocoa bean), sugar, vanilla and emulsifier, usually soya lecithin, to make plain chocolate. Milk chocolate has milk powder added as well. They are ground together to make a paste refined to grains no bigger than 17 microns – the tongue can detect nothing below 20 microns. All the machines are thickly coated with cream-coloured paint and have a vintage air, like a ship's engine room. It turns out they date from the 1960s. 'We bought modern ones, which were much more efficient, but they just didn't produce such good chocolate, so we went back to these,' explains Luce, as we head to the conching machines. These huge mixers stir the chocolate ingredients for up to three days, combining them at 60–70C and developing the flavours.

D But can a bar ever contain too much cocoa solids? I ask Pierre Costet, head taster for Valrhona, over a table of chocolate samples. 'Yes'. The blend of beans with cocoa butter and sugar should vary according to the subtleties of the flavour. Costet also believes the merits of the three varieties of cacao bean are exaggerated. It is widely accepted that Criollo (mostly from Venezuela) is the connoisseur's choice and Trinitario, grown in South and Central America, is the best mainstream variety. Forestero, grown in Africa, is considered coarse, mass-market stuff. This, Costet tells me, is too simplistic. First, because cacao trees are grown from seed by the farmers, they may have been cross-pollinated with the other varieties anyway. Second, how the beans are grown and fermented makes a huge difference, so a well-looked-after Forestero may well be better than a poorly treated Criollo.

WRITING 1 hour 30 minutes

PART 1

Read the two texts below.

Write an essay summarising and evaluating the key points from both texts. Use your own words throughout as far as possible, and include your own ideas in your answer.

Write your answer in 240–280 words.

1

Unsustainable tourism

We are increasingly familiar with some of the worst effects of unthinking, unmanaged, unsustainable tourism: previously undeveloped coastal villages that have become sprawling, charmless towns, their seas poisoned by sewage, denuded of wildlife, their beaches stained with litter and tubes of suncream; and historic towns, their streets now choked with traffic, their temples, churches and cathedrals seemingly reduced to a backdrop for holiday snaps that proclaim, 'Been there, Done that'. Less appreciated, perhaps, is the social dislocation unsustainable tourism can cause: once-cohesive communities disrupted as the holiday industry replaces old crafts, turning fishermen into tour boat operators and farmers into fast-food store waiters or hotel cleaners.

Criticism of the tourism industry

Although its strongest critics view the tourism industry as a rapacious predator – moving on to fresh conquests after one environment has been spoiled, and forever fuelling the desires of holidaymakers with the prospect of a new paradise that must be enjoyed 'before it's gone' – there are many within the industry who reject the claim. They are at least partly right. There are examples where the travel trade is doing better. Of course, reforming initiatives often come after the damage has been done and in some cases for public relations purposes rather than from a commitment to sustainability.

Write your essay.

NOTE: There is a sample answer to this question and assessment of it on page 126.

PART 2

Write an answer to one *of the questions 2–5 in this part. Write your answer in* 280–320 *words in an appropriate style.*

2   A magazine is running a competition for the best article entitled 'I Was There'. Those entering have to write an article describing an historical event as if they had been present at it. Write an article for this competition, describing the event you have chosen and what your impressions would have been if you had witnessed it.

Write your article.

3   You have been appointed as a student representative at your school or college. The head has asked you to write a report on what facilities and forms of entertainment the students would like to see introduced, based on a project you organize yourself to find out the opinions of students. Within your report, you should explain how you gathered the opinions and make recommendations as to what should be introduced and what benefits would result.

Write your report.

4   A TV listings magazine has invited readers to contribute a review of a television series that is or was particularly popular. Write a review, explaining why this programme is/was so popular in your opinion and commenting on whether you believe it deserves/deserved such popularity.

Write your review.

5   Set book questions – a choice from three questions.

NOTE: There is a sample answer for Question 4 and an assessment of it on page 126.

LISTENING   approx. 40 minutes

PART 1

You will hear three different extracts.
For questions 1–6, choose the answer (A, B or C) which fits best according to what you hear.
There are two questions for each extract.

___

Extract One
You hear the introduction to a radio programme about the arts and science in Britain.

1 What does the speaker say about the phrase 'The Two Cultures'?
   A Some people consider it no longer relevant.
   B It describes an undesirable situation.
   C It is used mostly by scientists.

2 The speaker regards C P Snow as someone who
   A attracted a certain amount of unfair criticism.
   B had ideas that were ahead of their time.
   C failed in his chosen fields of work.

Extract Two
You hear a travel agent talking about problems with customers.

3 What does she say about lost tickets?
   A There has been an increase in the number of them.
   B People make up reasons why they have been lost.
   C Some explanations given are easier to believe than others.

4 What does she suggest about the man travelling for heart surgery?
   A He could have been extremely angry when he returned.
   B He did well to sort out his own problem by himself.
   C What happened to him is unlikely to happen to anyone else.

Extract Three
You hear part of a radio programme about a British couple, Victoria and Mark, who make wildlife films in Africa.

5 Freddie got his nickname because
   A he can distinguish between different kinds of snake.
   B he appears to enjoy contact with snakes.
   C he is always pointing out snakes to other people.

6 When describing their current location, Mark emphasizes
   A how much it differs from his expectations of it.
   B how hard it is to predict weather conditions there.
   C how difficult their everyday life there is.

PART 2

You will hear someone called Kate Charters describing her career.
For questions 7–15, complete the sentences with a word or short phrase.

Kate's first job involved selling [_____ **7**] by phone.

Three years later, she started working for a company called [_____ **8**] .

When she joined Visnews, she first worked in the company's [_____ **9**] .

The videos made by Visnews were [_____ **10**] on topics of special interest.

The videos made by Visnews were sold in shops and by [_____ **11**] methods.

At Castle Communications, one 'side deal' involved holding a [_____ **12**] at a theme park.

She returned to Visnews and is currently in charge of its [_____ **13**] .

Kate's present job involves providing companies with the services of [_____ **14**] as well as with certain facilities and technology.

Throughout her career, she has been given valuable assistance by someone who is employed by a [_____ **15**] .

TEST 1

PART 3

You will hear an interview with a British politician.
For questions 16–20, choose the answer (A, B, C or D) which fits best according to what you hear.

16 Susan says that she particularly dislikes politicians who

    A   pretend to feel strongly about issues.

    B   disguise their real beliefs.

    C   are indecisive about issues.

    D   openly treat voters with contempt.

17 When she had her disagreement with Martin Jones, Susan

    A   decided that personal ambition was not her main motivation.

    B   began to feel that she had failed as a politician.

    C   felt that her point of view was not correctly understood.

    D   regretted the effect it would have on her future in politics.

18 What was Susan's attitude to involving colleagues in the controversy?

    A   She realized that they were unlikely to share her point of view.

    B   She was reluctant to do so because she was not sure she was right.

    C   She thought that involving colleagues would make things worse.

    D   She felt they should decide for themselves whether she had a point.

19 When asked whether her opinion of her colleagues has changed, Susan says that

    A   their reaction has made her reluctant to get into the same position again.

    B   she prefers those who criticized her to those who kept their opinions private.

    C   there may come a time when she does not publicly support them on issues.

    D   politicians place too much emphasis on their personal opinions of each other.

20 Susan thinks she was considered mad by some other politicians because

    A   her behaviour was out of character.

    B   they found her intimidating.

    C   she did not conform.

    D   her unselfishness shamed them.

PART 4

You will hear five short extracts in which people are talking about books they have read.
You will hear the recording twice.

TASK ONE

For questions 21–25, choose from the list (A–H) why each speaker read the book.

TASK TWO

For questions 26–30, choose from the list (A–H) each speaker's opinion of the book.

While you listen, you must complete both tasks.

A	personal recommendation	
B	desire for a change	
C	favourable reviews	
D	advertising	
E	gift	
F	keenness on the author	
G	to fill time	
H	interest in the subject	

Speaker 1		21
Speaker 2		22
Speaker 3		23
Speaker 4		24
Speaker 5		25

A	It is overrated.	
B	It is very entertaining.	
C	It is surprisingly good	
D	It requires effort.	
E	More people should read it.	
F	It is too long.	
G	It is thought-provoking.	
H	It deserves its success.	

Speaker 1		26
Speaker 2		27
Speaker 3		28
Speaker 4		29
Speaker 5		30

SPEAKING   16 minutes

Note: Assessment criteria are on page 93.

PART 2 (4 minutes)

Authority

A

B

C

D

PART 1 (2 minutes)

Questions that may be addressed to either candidate.

- Where are you from?
- Are you working or studying at the moment?
- What do you like most/least about your studies/job? (Why?)
- Describe briefly a typical day at college/school/university/work.
- Has your college/school/university/work changed since you started there?
- Who are your best friends?
- How did you meet your friends?
- What do you particularly like about your friends?
- What faults do any of your friends have?

PART 2 (4 minutes)   Authority

(Pictures are on page 24)

For both candidates

Here are some pictures of people doing various jobs. Look at pictures A and B and talk together about the good and bad aspects of these jobs for the people who do them.
(Candidates A and B: 1 minute)

Now look at all the pictures.

Imagine that you are going to take part in a project about authority figures in your society and how much respect people in general have for them. These pictures show some of the authority figures that the project will focus on.

Talk together about attitudes that people have towards these authority figures. Then decide which of the authority figures is most respected in your society.
(Candidates A and B: 3 minutes)

PART 3 (10 minutes)   Effort and Reward

Task (a)

Candidate A (2 minutes)	**Do some people get paid a lot more/less than they deserve?** ■ overpaid/underpaid jobs ■ reasons why overpaid/underpaid ■ what the jobs really involve
Candidate B (1 minute)	**What jobs are generally regarded as desirable in your society? (Why?)** ■ Would you like to do any of these jobs? (Why?/Why not?) ■ What kind of jobs do people in your society not want to do? (Why?) *Candidate A: Do you agree?/What do you think?/How about you?*

Task (b)

Candidate B (2 minutes)	**Which jobs are the most difficult?** ■ most difficult aspects ■ how people doing them are generally regarded ■ importance of the jobs in society
Candidate A (1 minute)	■ What makes people want to do the difficult jobs in society? ■ What kind of person do you have to be to do such jobs? ■ Do you think you would be capable of doing any of them? ... (Why?/Why not?) *Candidate A: Do you agree?/What do you think?/How about you?*

Discussion

■ Have you done something where the effort was not worth it for the reward?
■ What motivation do people in general have in their jobs?
■ What expectations do young people have regarding effort and reward? (Why?)
■ How are successful people regarded in your society?
■ Is there a particular job which you think deserves to be much more highly paid than it is? (Why?)
■ Which jobs are the most highly respected in your society?

(Candidate A and B: 4 minutes)

READING & USE OF ENGLISH   1 hour 30 minutes

For questions 1–8, read the text below and decide which answer (A, B, C or D) best fits each gap. Mark your answers on the separate answer sheet.

There is an example at the beginning (0).

Example:

0 A land   **B** line   **C** sort   **D** fall

0	A	B	C	D

Travel Books of the Year

The best travel books of this year **0** _____D_____ into three main categories; purely informational, narrative, and what, for **1** _____ of a better term, I'll call 'anecdotal'. Between these broad categories, however, the boundaries are **2** _____ . One problem with putting travel writers into genres is that they are **3** _____ to be pigeon-holed. Many of them see their role as a **4** _____ of the documentary and the creative.

Some **5** _____ to be more like novelists, **6** _____ some of the elements of fiction writing. Others regard themselves as sociologists, exploring the customs and mores of other societies. At the end of the day, what **7** _____ is how readable or useful the book is, and in many cases, how well it is presented. However, it is quite clear that travel and books were **8** _____ for each other.

1 A want	**B** absence	**C** shortage	**D** need
2 A misted	**B** blurred	**C** blended	**D** sketchy
3 A wary	**B** loath	**C** cautious	**D** resistant
4 A merger	**B** mixture	**C** cross	**D** compound
5 A allege	**B** hold	**C** claim	**D** contend
6 A engaging	**B** exerting	**C** employing	**D** exercising
7 A counts	**B** reckons	**C** bears	**D** signifies
8 A given	**B** cut	**C** lent	**D** made

PART 2

For questions 9–16, read the text below and think of the word which best fits each gap. Use only one word in each gap. There is an example at the beginning (0). Write your answers IN CAPITAL LETTERS on the separate answer sheet.

Example:

| 0 | T | H | E | I | R | | | | | | | | |

THE CULT OF CELEBRITY

Once, children had ambitions to be doctors, explorers, sportsmen, artists or scientists. Now, taking
0 __their__ lead from TV, they just 'want to be famous'. Fame is no longer a reward for gallant
service or great, perhaps even selfless endeavour. It is an end in 9_____ , and the sooner it can be
achieved, the sooner the lonely bedroom mirror can be replaced by the TV camera and flash gun, the
10_____ .

Celebrity is the profession of the moment, a vainglorious vocation which seems to exist largely
11_____ that the rest of us might watch and be amazed as its members live out their lives in public,
like self-regarding members of some glittering soap opera. Today, almost 12_____ can be famous.
Never has fame 13_____ more democratic, more ordinary, more achievable. 14_____ wonder
it's a modern ambition. Modern celebrity, peopled by 15_____ largely vain and vacuous, fills a need
in our lives. It peoples talk shows, sells goods and newspapers and rewards the famous for – well,
16_____ famous.

PART 3

For questions 17–24, read the text below. Use the word given in capitals at the end of some of the lines to form a word that fits in the gap in the same line. There is an example at the beginning (0). Write your answers IN CAPITAL LETTERS on the separate answer sheet.

Example:

| 0 | S | P | E | C | T | A | C | U | L | A | R | | | |

SKIING HOLIDAYS IN COLORADO

To ski or snowboard in Colorado is to experience the pinnacle of winter

sports. The state of Colorado is known for its **0** _spectacular_ scenery and   **SPECTACLE**

17 _____ views, which inspire today's travellers as much as they   **BREATH**

spurred on the **18** _____ who first arrived in this part of the US over   **SETTLE**

a century ago. And whether you're seeking the outdoor adventure of a

19 _____ , exciting nightlife or a great family getaway, Colorado has   **LIFE**

everything you need.

November through April, snow conditions are **20** _____ and reliable,   **CONSIST**

featuring Colorado's **21** _____ 'champagne powder' snow. Extensive   **LEGEND**

snowmaking and grooming operations always keep trails in top shape.

The mountain destinations in the Colorado Rockies can turn your wildest ski

dreams into thrilling **22** _____ . There, you'll find the best skiing and   **REAL**

snowboarding on **23** _____ slopes, as well as the finest ski schools in the   **PICTURE**

US. Together, they present an **24** _____ winter paradise.   **PARALLEL**

PART 4

For questions 25–30, complete the second sentence so that it has a similar meaning to the first sentence, using the word given. Do not change the word given. You must use between three and eight words, including the word given. Here is an example (0):

Example:

0   Dan definitely won't be able to afford a holiday this year.

   possiblity

   There _____ to afford a holiday this year.

0	is no possibility of Dan being able

Write only the missing words on the separate answer sheet.

___

25   I always enjoy this film, no matter how often I see it.

   tire

   However _____ this film.

26   I don't know why Fred made such an extraordinary decision.

   prompted

   I don't know _____ a decision.

27 Inefficient treatment of customers creates a bad impression of the company.

reflects

Treating customers with a lack _____ the company.

28 The organizers planned everything as carefully as they could possibly have done.

utmost

Everything was planned _____ by the organizers.

29 I promised him that the situation would not be repeated in the future.

word

I _____ no repetition of the situation in the future.

30 Tim tried to be like one of his heroes when he was a young musician.

modelled

As _____ one of his heroes.

PART 5

Parenthood

Paul watched the television above the bar. An army of turtles waddled up a beach, cumbersome helmets dragged through the fine sand to deposit a clutch of smooth, white eggs in the dunes. He saw the wriggling reptilian babies emerge sticky from the broken shells and repeat the journey in reverse, thousands of tiny helmets trundling inexorably over the moonlit dunes towards the breakers. Those who escaped being flipped over on their backs and pecked to death by wading birds were finally swallowed up in the surf. There was no pleasure involved in this reptilian cycle of birth and death. The turtles survived purely because there were so many of them, and the oceans were so vast, that one or two were bound to slip through unnoticed.

He wondered why they bothered, and presumed it could only be because they had no choice. Their genes forced them ever onwards – life would not be denied. Previous generations had imposed their will upon their distant descendants, and the descendants wearily obeyed. If, by chance, a turtle was born in whom this instinct towards multiplication was misformed or absent, a turtle whose instincts directed them not towards reproduction but towards reflection on the purpose of reproduction, say, or towards seeing how long it could stay underwater on one breath, then this instinct would die with the turtle. The turtles were condemned to multiply purely by the breeding success of their own ancestors. There was no escape for them. Multiplication, once set in motion, was unstoppable.

At the present moment, the balance of his own inclinations tilted more towards sleep, the cessation of thought, hibernation, vegetation. Had he been one of those tiny helmets, he would, at that moment, have flipped over belly-up in the sand and simply awaited the releasing beak. Parenthood had taken him by surprise. The books, the articles, the classes, had not prepared him for the intensity of it all. Snap decisions to be made, everybody looking to him for the answers, and no way of knowing if he had made the correct guess, no way of finding his way back to the main track if he took a wrong turning. Last night he had been half a couple. He had lived with others all his life. It was easy – you had rows, you had resentments, but if they became too frequent or too boring, or if the compensations ceased to be adequate, you just left, and tried again with someone else until you found someone you could put up with. He could not remember how it had all changed. Perhaps it had been the doors of youth and liberty creaking shut behind him, or the demands that were suddenly being made of him, the faces turning towards him when a decision was required. Or perhaps it was just the steaming concoction of his emotions, his hormones, his thoughts slopping around his veins with the coffee and nicotine. Whatever it was, something had obliged him to seek out a tranquil place in order to restore some order to his metabolism.

Then there was the feeling that he had been duped – the one feeling that he hadn't been warned of – when he saw mother and baby together and realized that the reason why everyone made such a big deal of fatherhood these days was simply because it was such an implausible state. Mothers and babies were the world. Fathers were optional extras, accessories. If some strange virus colonized the Y-chromosome and poisoned all the men, the world would carry on. It would not be a very exciting world perhaps, rather bland and predictable, but women would find some way to reproduce, and within a generation or two it would be difficult to believe that there had ever been men at all. They would appear in the encyclopaedias somewhere between dinosaurs and Romans. Future generations of little girls would try, in vain, to understand what it had been that men had done, how they had contributed. What use had they been? He had suddenly seen his role exposed as that of a footnote. The books had warned him of this feeling, of jealousy, of irrelevance and superfluity. They had said it was natural, that he would get over it. What they had not said was that it was natural because it was so manifestly, poignantly true, or that he would get over it only by stopping thinking about it. Fathers deceived themselves. Mothers and babies held it all together. The men came and went, interchangeably, causing trouble and bringing presents to make up for it.

31 What did Paul notice about the turtles in the first paragraph?

    A their reluctance to return to the sea

    B their behaviour with their young

    C the effort they made to survive

    D the tiny proportion of young who survived

32 Paul assumed that if a turtle did not wish to reproduce,

    A it would be punished by other turtles.

    B it would end up doing so anyway.

    C this attitude would not spread to other turtles.

    D this would not come as a surprise.

33 His thoughts turned towards going to sleep because

    A he knew that he was unlikely to get much in the near future.

    B he had been left mentally exhausted by becoming a parent.

    C he had become weary of his actions being criticized.

    D he felt that that was what many of the turtles probably wanted to do.

34 What did he feel he had been forced to do since last night?

    A accept that he was not really cut out for living with other people

    B find a way of making himself feel better physically

    C identify precisely what had caused his life to change so radically

    D remind himself of how he had felt prior to this

35 In what way did he feel that he had been duped?

    A He had expected his role to be one that differed from that of most men.

    B He had not been informed about how women changed when they became mothers.

    C He had not been told the truth by women about how they really regarded men.

    D He had thought fatherhood was treated as a major subject because fathers were important.

36 He felt that the books had failed to warn him that his feeling of irrelevance

    A would not fade away naturally.

    B would not be shared by others.

    C would be replaced by worse feelings.

    D would reduce him to inactivity.

You are going to read an extract from a book. Seven paragraphs have been removed from the extract. Choose from the paragraphs A–H the one which fits each gap (37–43). There is one extra paragraph which you do not use. Mark your answers on the separate answer sheet.

The football club Chairman

Bryan Richardson greeted me warmly, and ushered me into his modest office, somewhat larger than the others along the corridor, but without pretensions of any kind. He returned to his desk, which had two phones and a mobile on it, and a lot of apparently unsorted papers, offered me a chair, and said it was nice to see me again. I rather doubt he remembered me at all, but it had the effect of making me feel a little less anxious.

37

'I want to talk to you about an idea I have,' I said. 'I have supported this club since the 1970s, and I'm starting to get frustrated by watching so much and knowing so little.' He gazed at me with a degree of interest mixed with incomprehension. 'What I mean,' I added, 'is that every football fan is dying to know what it is really like, what's actually going on, yet all we get to see is what happens on the field.'

38

And I didn't wish to be fobbed off. 'They all make it worse, not better. They all purvey gossip and rumours, and most of what they say turns out to be either uninteresting or incorrect. Your average supporter ends up in the dark most of the time.'

39

'Now that,' I said, 'is just the sort of thing I want to know about. I'd like to write a book about the club this coming season, to know about the deals, the comings and goings, all the factors involved. To get to know how a Premiership football club actually works.' As I said this, I feared that it was a futile request, but I'd drawn a little hope from the fact that he had just been so open, as if he had already decided to consider the project. 'I want to know about buying and selling players, how the finances work, to go down to the training ground, travel with the team, talk to the players and the manager.'

40

So I continued with it. 'Let me tell you a little about myself.' He leaned back to make himself comfortable, sensing that this might take a while. 'By training I'm an academic. I came here from America in the 1960s, got a doctorate in English at Oxford, then taught in the English Department at Warwick University for fifteen years. Now I run my own business, dealing in rare books and manuscripts in London, and do some freelance writing. But I'm not a journalist.'

41

I was starting to babble now, and as I spoke I was aware of how foolish all this must be sounding to him. At one point he put his hands quietly on his lap, under the desk, and I had the distinct, if paranoid, impression that he was ringing some sort of hidden alarm, and that three orange-shirted stewards would shortly come in and escort me from the ground (By Order of the Chairman).

42

'But a book is certainly a good idea,' he said. 'Let me think it over and I'll get back to you.' He stood up and we shook hands. 'I'll be in touch,' he said. And a few weeks later, in mid-August, he was. 'There's a great story here,' he said. 'Go ahead and do it next season. I'll introduce you to the people up here at the club. Go everywhere, talk to everybody, you'll find it fascinating.' I was surprised, and delighted, but tried not to gush. 'Thank you,' I said. 'It's very open-minded of you.'

43

'Yes, sure,' he said. 'But I mean something more than that, something more complicated.' 'What's that?' I asked. He smiled. 'You'll see.'

A The disappointment must have registered on my face, because he quickly added: 'I came to all this relatively late in my career, and it's a fascinating business. I find it more so all the time, and I don't have any doubt that people would be interested to read an account of it.'

B 'We've got nothing to hide,' he said, 'but you'll be surprised by what you learn. It's an amazingly emotional business.' 'It must be,' I said, 'the supporters can see that. So many of the games are like an emotional rollercoaster. Sometimes the whole season is.'

C He nodded gently. 'Good,' he said firmly. 'That's part of the point,' I went on. 'I want to write about the club from the point of view of the supporters, a sort of fan's eye view. Getting behind the scenes is every fan's dream – whether it's here or somewhere else. I've never written anything like this, although I have written a couple of books. And I am trained, as an academic, in habits of analysis, in trying to figure out how things work. And I'm a supporter of the club, so I don't think there is anything to fear.'

D As I was speaking, the mobile phone rang, and he answered it with an apologetic shrug. A brief and cryptic one-sided conversation ensued, with obscure references to hotels and phone numbers. When he hung up, he explained: 'We're trying to sign a full-back. Good player. But there are three agents involved, and two continental sides want to sign him, so we've got him hidden in a hotel. If we can keep them away from him for another couple of days, he'll sign.'

E He considered this for a moment. 'Well,' he said, 'there is the ClubCall line, the match-day programmes, and the articles in the local and national papers. There's lots of information about.' He sounded like a politician trying to claim for his party the moral authority of open government, while at the same time giving nothing away.

F Not at all. 'It's funny you should ask,' he said, 'because you're the second person this week who has come in with a request to write a book about the club. And I've just been approached by the BBC with a proposal to do a six-part documentary about the club. 'Are you going to let them do it?' I asked. 'I don't think,' he said wryly, 'that a six-part series on what a nice club Coventry City is would make good television.'

G 'So, what can I do for you?' He made it sound as if he were interested. Poised and well dressed, though without foppishness, he had that indefinable polish that one often observes in people of wealth or celebrity. By polish I do not mean good manners, though that frequently accompanies it, but something more tangible: a kind of glow, as if the rich and famous applied some mysterious ointment (available only to themselves) every morning, and then buffed their faces to a healthy sheen.

H There, I'd done it. The worst that he could do was to tell me to get lost. Part of me, to tell the truth, would have been just a little relieved. But he didn't do anything. He sat quite still, listening, letting me make my pitch.

You are going to read an extract from an article about the relationship between movement and health. For questions 44–53, choose from the sections (A–D). The sections may be chosen more than once. Mark your answers **on the separate answer sheet.**

In which section are the following mentioned?

a cautious reaction to some information	**44**
the reason for the decrease in the amount of movement made by people	**45**
the solution to a problem in carrying out some research	**46**
information from which it was initially hard to draw a conclusion	**47**
a gradual acceptance of the connection between movement and health	**48**
something widely acknowledged but not acted upon	**49**
proof that not everyone regarded an idea as ridiculous	**50**
a finding that pleased the person who made it	**51**
a history of taking an unusual approach to research	**52**
a view that could be regarded as too extreme	**53**

Keep Moving

A In 2006, James Levine, a scientist based at the Mayo Clinic in Minnesota, conducted a very strange experiment. He wanted to measure something which goes by the cumbersome title of Non-Exercise Activity Thermogenesis – or NEAT. Essentially, this examines how people move about during an average day – not when they're exercising, but when they're making no special effort to keep fit. The big question was just how to do the measuring – and here Levine hit upon a radical plan. He decided to put his volunteers into specially sensored underwear. This would measure their every waking and sleeping moment. Levine, incidentally, is no stranger to weird experiments. Aged 10, he'd placed 15 pond snails in a glass tank and tracked their movements every hour across a piece of wax paper. Twelve months and 200 wax paper trials later, he came to the same conclusion that he reached 23 years later in his sensored underwear experiment. All creatures have a biological imperative to move – and movement, perhaps more than anything else, is good for us.

B By the same token, lack of movement is very bad indeed. The NEAT experiment revealed that lean people burn around 350 more calories a day just by fidgeting, pacing about, or walking to the coffee machine. As for the non-lean ones, they just sat there, getting ever more bloated and unfit. Sitting down, Levine concluded, is not just bad for people – it's a killer. This may seem a bit drastic, but Levine isn't the only scientist who reckons that being sedentary offers an accelerated route to an early grave. However, the vast majority of us move about less and less. As labour-intensive jobs disappear, we live in an increasingly sedentary world, spending our working lives stuck in a chair and ever larger amounts of our leisure time too. We know that exercise is good for us and that sitting down all day isn't – we just choose to ignore it.

C Soon after the end of the Second World War, a British health researcher called Jerry Morris set up a study to examine why record numbers of people were dying of heart attacks. The first results Morris got in were from London busmen. Immediately, he saw that there was a striking difference: drivers were twice as likely to suffer a heart attack as conductors. To begin with, this didn't make sense. After all, they were much the same age, ate much the same food and so on. There was only one key difference. Whereas the drivers spent their days behind the wheel, conductors spent theirs running up and down the stairs. Morris thought he might be on to something, but it was still too early to say: he had to wait for other data to arrive. Then came the figures for postal workers. These were strikingly similar to the bus drivers: the postmen who delivered the mail by bike and on foot had markedly fewer heart attacks than the ones who served behind counters. His paper, 'Coronary Heart-disease and Physical Activity of Work', was published in 1953 – and greeted with hoots of derision by his peers. But Morris, as people slowly began to concede, was onto something.

D Two hundred years ago, people may have led much less sedentary lives, but they still had an inkling that sitting down wasn't doing them any good. No one seems to know exactly when the standing desk was invented, but by the mid 19th century, they were a regular fixture in the offices and homes of the rich. But if people could get used to working standing up, could they go one step further? One evening in 2007, Levine was in his office thinking about the relationship between exercise and fitness when he had an idea. Instead of people nipping off to the gym and then coming back to slump at their desks, maybe they could exercise at the same time as working. Sliding a hospital tray on top of a treadmill, Levine set it to a modest 2mph. To his surprise, he found he could work perfectly easily while he was walking along. He could type, make phone calls and do almost everything that he normally did sitting down. Yet after an hour, he'd burned off more than 100 calories. It was, as he admits, an eccentric invention. 'There was a notion floating about that I had completely flipped.' But television stations began doing news reports, and all at once people didn't think he was so nutty after all. Soon, the treadmill desk, or Walkstation as it was called, had gone into commercial production.

WRITING   1 hour 30 minutes

PART 1

Read the two texts below.

Write an essay summarising and evaluating the key points from both texts. Use your own words throughout as far as possible, and include your own ideas in your answer.

Write your answer in **240–280 words.**

1

The birth of 'youth culture'

In the early 1960s, a new wave of romantic enthusiasm and innovation – political, spiritual and cultural, or rather, countercultural – broke over the Western world. At first, only a few social and aesthetic radicals were involved in what presently came to be called the Youth Culture. The majority of right-thinking persons were offended or bored by the new music, the new art and the new politics, but a shrewd student of fashion, observing what was being worn on the streets of Europe and America, might have predicted that in a few years youth would be adored and emulated everywhere; that, indeed, simply to be under 30 would be accounted a virtue.

What is 'youth culture'?

It has been argued that the 'youth culture' that began in the 1960s was the product of manipulation of impressionable young people by commercial interests, that youth culture is really no more than the range of products available specifically for the young. Others have tried to explain youth subcultures, not in terms of mindless consumption but in terms of genuine style innovation, and the generation of styles which 'say' something about the social and economic conditions in which those young people live, their experiences and their aspirations.

Write your essay.

Write an answer to one of the questions 2–5 in this part. Write your answer in 280–320 words in an appropriate style.

2   You are employed as a researcher by a television company that is preparing a documentary about the social problems in your area or country. You have been told to write a report on the problems that you think the programme should cover. Write your report, listing the problems and describing the causes and consequences of them which you think the programme should highlight.

Write your **report**.

3   An arts magazine has invited readers to send in reviews of a concert, show or play which pleasantly surprised, or disappointed them. Write a review, describing the concert, show or play and saying how it differed from your expectations of it and what had caused you to have those expectations.

Write your **review**.

4   You are staying in another country where you have read an article in a magazine about a custom there that the writer considers strange. Write a letter to the magazine, describing a custom or customs in your own country that may be considered strange by outsiders and giving your own views and those of others in your country about it.

Write your **letter**.

5   Set book questions – a choice from three questions.

NOTE: There is a sample answer for Question 2 and an assessment of it on page 127.

LISTENING approx. 40 minutes

PART 1

You will hear three different extracts.
For questions 1–6, choose the answer (A, B or C) which fits best according to what you hear.
There are two questions for each extract.

Extract One
You hear part of a radio programme about courses for women.

1 The presenter says that the car maintenance course
   A is chiefly aimed at women with cars in bad condition.
   B may not produce the same results for everyone who takes it.
   C is essential for women who get upset if their cars do not work properly.

2 Helen says that one result of taking the course is that
   A she can repair most faults with her car herself.
   B she no longer runs the risk of being cheated by mechanics.
   C she can prevent certain problems with her car from occurring.

Extract Two
You hear a receptionist talking about callers she has to deal with.

3 When people tell her that she is unlikely to be able to help them, she
   A criticizes them for their attitude.
   B tells them that they may well be right.
   C promises to make a special effort on their behalf.

4 When callers continue a conversation with someone else, she
   A is tempted to do something that might be considered rude.
   B finds some of the things they say quite amusing.
   C knows they are unlikely to have a sensible question for her.

Extract Three
You hear the introduction to a radio programme about food in Britain.

5 The speaker says that it is typical of English people to
   A look for unusual places to have picnics.
   B have picnics they do not appear to enjoy.
   C take the wrong kind of food for picnics.

6 While describing the history of picnics, the speaker
   A refers to the image that the sandwich has acquired.
   B expresses surprise that they became traditional in Britain.
   C points out that they have increased in popularity over the ages.

PART 2

You will hear part of a radio interview with a diver.
For questions 7–15, complete the sentences with a word or short phrase.

John's first experience of diving involved putting a [_____ 7] round his body.

He says that years ago, diving could be compared with [_____ 8] .

The diving equipment he had in the Army had previously been used for [_____ 9] .

John is not comfortable when he is near to [_____ 10] .

John's worst mistake happened when he was trying to recover a very old [_____ 11] .

When he got to the surface on that occasion, he had problems with his [_____] and his [_____ 12] .

Another bad experience happened when he was trying to lift a [_____ 13] that was stuck in mud.

While testing a device in Florida, he crashed into the [_____ 14] .

These days, he is very keen on the [_____ 15] aspect of diving.

You will hear part of a radio phone-in programme about consumer competitions that appear in magazines or are run by shops, in which advice is given to people who regularly enter them.
For questions 16–20, choose the answer (A, B, C or D) which fits best according to what you hear.

16 Diana has phoned because she

    A feels that she is the victim of an injustice.

    B is reluctant to consult a lawyer yet.

    C fears she misunderstood an agreement she made.

    D wants to avoid falling out with her best friend.

17 Kathy tells Diana that

    A her problem is a rather unusual one.

    B she should have been more careful when dealing with her friend.

    C it is unfortunate that her friend has the attitude that she has.

    D she would regret taking legal action.

18 What does Kathy tell Ron about using different names when entering competitions?

    A People who do so are regularly caught out.

    B It may affect the quality of a competitor's entries.

    C There are rarely occasions when it might be justified.

    D It is unusual for competitors to decide to do so.

19 What has led Stan to phone in?

    A an inadequate response to a complaint he has made

    B a feeling of confusion as to the rules of a competition

    C a belief that he has been sent inaccurate information

    D a desire for more openness about the results of competitions

20 What does Kathy tell Stan about the competition he entered?

    A Some of the phrasing of the instructions is ambiguous.

    B The rules allow for results that may appear unfair.

    C A deliberate attempt has been made to mislead competitors.

    D It is the sort of competition that it is best not to enter.

PART 4

You will hear five short extracts in which people are talking about their day at work.
You will hear the recording twice.

TASK ONE

For questions 21–25, choose from the list (A–H) what happened at work.

TASK TWO

For questions 26–30, choose from the list (A–H) each speaker's feeling about what happened.

While you listen, you must complete both tasks.

A	an unexpected problem	
B	an appraisal	Speaker 1 21
C	a disagreement with a colleague	Speaker 2 22
D	an unexpected opportunity	Speaker 3 23
E	a successful meeting	Speaker 4 24
F	a bad mistake	Speaker 5 25
G	wasted effort	
H	criticism from a manager	

A	furious	
B	worried	Speaker 1 26
C	impressed	Speaker 2 27
D	confused	Speaker 3 28
E	guilty	Speaker 4 29
F	relaxed	Speaker 5 30
G	suspicious	
H	optimistic	

SPEAKING   16 minutes

Note: Assessment criteria are on page 93.

PART 2   (4 minutes)

Ambition

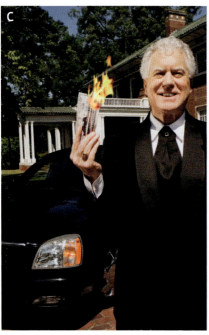

PART 1 (2 minutes)

Questions that may be addressed to either candidate.

■ Where are you from?
■ Are you working or studying at the moment?
■ Why is English an important language to learn these days?
■ What is the attitude to learning foreign languages in general in your country?
■ What have you found most difficult about learning English?
■ What have you enjoyed most about learning English?
■ What forms of entertainment do you prefer (TV, cinema, music, reading, etc.)?
■ Describe briefly your favourite film.
■ What kind(s) of TV programme do you enjoy watching?

PART 2 (4 minutes)   Ambition

(Pictures are on page 44)

For both candidates

Here are some pictures of people who have achieved their ambitions. Look at pictures A and B and talk together about the different ambitions that they illustrate.
(Candidates A and B: 1 minute)

Now look at all the pictures.

Imagine that you have been asked to write an article for a website about the kind of ambitions that young people have today. These pictures are being considered as illustrations of your main point in the article.

Talk together about how common the ambitions shown in the pictures are for young people today. Then decide which picture illustrates the most common ambition of young people today.
(Candidates A and B: 3 minutes)

(10 minutes)   Truth and Dishonesty

Task (a)

Candidate A (2 minutes)	**Can it ever be justifiable to tell a lie to friends / family?** ■ circumstances in which people most often lie ■ what kind of lies they tell ■ good / bad results of lying
Candidate B (1 minute)	■ What were you told as a child about lying? ■ In what circumstances would you never lie? ■ What kind of lies do you think are not serious/bad ones? *Candidate A: Do you agree?/What do you think?/How about you?*

Task (b)

Candidate B (2 minutes)	**What kinds of people are the most dishonest in society?** ■ jobs that involve lying ■ the effects on society of this dishonesty ■ how much people believe these lies
Candidate A (1 minute)	■ In what circumstances might you say something dishonest? ■ What kind of problems can honesty cause? ■ Do you think you are good at lying? (Why? / Why not?) *Candidate A: Do you agree?/What do you think?/How about you?*

Discussion

■ What kinds of lies cause the most trouble for other people? (Why?)
■ Would you tell a lie in order to help someone else? (Why? / Why not?)
■ What indications do people give that they are lying?
■ What is your attitude towards people who cheat in games?
■ Why might someone want to believe something that is not true?
■ What can people gain from telling lies?

(Candidate A and B: 4 minutes)

READING & USE OF ENGLISH   1 hour 30 minutes

PART 1

For questions 1–8, read the text below and decide which answer (A, B, C or D) best fits each gap. Mark your answers on the separate answer sheet.

There is an example at the beginning (0).

Example:

0   A compelled   **B** enforced   **C** necessitated   **D** restricted

0	A	B	C	D

The Journey

The car had again failed to start, and Elizabeth was again **0** ____A____ to take the train. She brought a cup of coffee down the rocking carriage, **1**_____ as the boiling fluid seeped out from under the lid and on to her hand. The heating was turned up **2**_____ and most of the people in the carriage seemed on the **3**_____ of unconsciousness as they looked out of the window at the flatlands sliding **4**_____ the window. Elizabeth had telephoned the matron of the home, who told her that Brennan was barely worth visiting, but that he would see her if she came. She felt excited by the **5**_____ of actually meeting someone from that era. She would be like a historian who, after working from other histories, finally **6**_____ hands on original source material. She had an unclear **7**_____ of Brennan in her mind, although she knew he would be old and, **8**_____ from what the matron had said, decrepit.

1	**A** leering	**B** squinting	**C** wincing	**D** smirking
2	**A** top	**B** full	**C** maximum	**D** peak
3	**A** verge	**B** rim	**C** fringe	**D** border
4	**A** beside	**B** along	**C** past	**D** across
5	**A** prospect	**B** outlook	**C** foresight	**D** viewpoint
6	**A** sets	**B** rests	**C** casts	**D** lays
7	**A** sight	**B** picture	**C** vision	**D** figure
8	**A** reflecting	**B** accounting	**C** judging	**D** rating

PART 2

For questions 9–16, read the text below and think of the word which best fits each gap. Use only one word in each gap. There is an example at the beginning (0).
Write your answers **IN CAPITAL LETTERS on the separate answer sheet.**

Example:

0	A	N	D										

THE ISLAND WHERE DREAMS CAME TRUE

Ellis Island in New York – that extraordinary entrance to a new land **0** __*and*__ a new life which received, processed and despatched millions of arriving immigrants **9** _____ 1892 and 1924 – has been turned into a museum. **10** _____ lain derelict for years after its official closure, the island's huge purpose-built reception centre has been restored. It has become a place of pilgrimage for the descendants of the desperate people who filed through its cavernous main hall to answer questions and **11** _____ in the forms in whatever halting English **12** _____ possessed.

To get to Ellis Island, you take a ferry from the southernmost tip of Manhattan. **13** _____ you sail past the Statue of Liberty and pull up to the dock outside the enormous entrance to that imposing reception building, it is impossible **14** _____ to reflect on **15** _____ it must have looked to those hordes of people who clambered off the boats with their children clinging **16** _____ them and their belongings packed into baskets and bags.

PART 3

For questions 17–24, read the text below. Use the word given in capitals at the end of some of the lines to form a word that fits in the gap in the same line. There is an example at the beginning (0). Write your answers IN CAPITAL LETTERS on the separate answer sheet.

Example:

| 0 | C | O | U | R | T | E | O | U | S | | | |

BOOK PUBLICISTS

The **0** *courteous* smile of an author selling books, signing copies or chatting   **COURTESY**

on television shows can be **17** _____ . Behind the scenes of the book tour   **DECEIVE**

that has become as much a part of the modern bestseller as print and paper,

the writer may be a **18** _____ for a Golden Dartboard Award. This is   **CONTEND**

the Oscar for authors **19** _____ behaving badly, an informal award   **ALLEGE**

nominated by the weary, sometimes **20** _____ , publicists who travel   **TRAUMA**

from city to city garnering publicity and sales. They call themselves 'babysitters'

as they tend to the fragile egos and **21** _____ demands of authors.   **CONVENTION**

Among the most feared **22** _____ for the publicists are the feminist writer   **ASSIGN**

who is remembered for yelling at her publicists in public and in **23** _____   **COLOUR**

language, and the thriller writer whose publicists report that they have

instructions from his publisher to speak only when spoken to. One **24** _____   **SURVIVE**

of a tour with him, who nominated him for a Golden Dartboard, says: 'He treats

us all as his inferiors.'

For questions **25–30**, complete the second sentence so that it has a similar meaning to the first sentence, using the word given. **Do not change the word given.** You must use between three and eight words, including the word given. Here is an example **(0):**

Example:

0 Dan definitely won't be able to afford a holiday this year.

   possiblity

   There _____ to afford a holiday this year.

0	is no possibility of Dan being able

Write only the missing words on the separate answer sheet.

---

25 Diane finds that creating things stops her from thinking about her work.

   mind

   Diane finds that being _____ her work.

26 I tried not to get involved in that situation.

   mixed

   I tried to avoid _____ that situation.

27 After announcing his resignation, he said that he had done nothing improper.

deny

After announcing his resignation, he went _____
improper.

28 I had to go to an expert and ask her to advise me.

seek

I was forced _____ expert.

29 I realized that I was in a terrible position and I wasn't to blame for it.

fault

Through _____ myself in a terrible position.

30 Francis chose computing rather than marketing for his next course.

preference

Francis opted _____ marketing for his next course.

PART 5

You are going to read an extract from a biography of two British comedians. For questions 31–36, choose the answer (A, B, C or D) which you think fits best according to the text. Mark your answers on the separate answer sheet.

The Morecambe & Wise Show

It happened one night. It happened, to be precise, at 8.55 p.m. on the night of 25 December 1977, when an estimated 28,835,000 people – more than half of the total population of the United Kingdom – tuned their television sets to BBC1 and spent the next hour and ten minutes in the company of a rather tall man called Eric and a rather short man called Ernie. It was an extraordinary night for British television. It was – at least as far as that catholic and capacious category known as 'light entertainment' was concerned – as close as British television had ever come, in some forty-one years of trying, to being a genuine mass medium. None of the usual rigid divisions and omissions were apparent in the broad audience of that remarkable night: no stark class bias, no pronounced gender imbalance, no obvious age asymmetry, no generalized demographic slant.

It was also, of course, an extraordinary night for the two stars of the show: Eric Morecambe and Ernie Wise – by far the most illustrious, and the best-loved, double-act that Britain has ever produced. Exceptionally professional yet endearingly personable, they were wonderful together as partners, as friends, as almost a distinct entity: not 'Morecambe and Wise' but 'Morecambewise'. There was Eric and there was Ernie: one of them an idiot, the other a bigger idiot, each of them half a star, together a whole star, forever hopeful of that 'brand new, bright tomorrow' that they sang about at the end of each show. True, Eric would often slap Ernie smartly on the cheeks, but they clearly thought the world of each other, and the world thought a great deal of them, too.

Their show succeeded in attracting such a massive following on that memorable night because it had, over the course of the previous nine years or so, established, and then enhanced, an enviable reputation for consistency, inventiveness, unparalleled professional polish and, last but by no means least, a strong and sincere respect for its audience. *The Morecambe & Wise Show* stood for something greater, something far more precious, than mere first-rate but evanescent entertainment; it had come to stand – just as persuasively and as proudly as any earnest documentary or any epic drama – for excellence in broadcasting, the result not just of two gifted performers (great talent, alas, does not of itself guarantee great television) but also of a richly proficient and supremely committed production team.

The show, culminating in the record-breaking triumph of that 1977 special, represented an achievement in high-quality popular programme-making that is now fast assuming the aura of a fairy tale – destined, one fears, to be passed on with bemused fascination from one doubtful generation to its even more disbelieving successor as the seemingly endless proliferation of new channels and novel forms of distraction continue to divide and disperse the old mass audience in the name of that remorseless quest for 'quality demographics' and 'niche audiences'. *The Morecambe & Wise Show* appeared at a time before home video, before satellite dishes and cable technology, before the dawning of the digital revolution, a time when it was still considered desirable to make a television programme that might – just might – excite most of the people most of the time.

Neither Morecambe nor Wise ever looked down on, or up at, anyone (except, of course, each other); both of them looked straight back at their audience on level terms. No celebrated guest was ever allowed to challenge this comic democracy: within the confines of the show, the rich and famous went unrecognised and frequently unpaid (a running gag); venerable actors with grand theatrical reputations were mocked routinely by Eric's *sotto voce* comments; and two resolutely down-to-earth working-class comedians gleefully reaffirmed the remarkably deep, warm and sure relationship that existed between themselves and the British public.

'It was,' reminisced Ernie Wise, 'a sort of great big office party for the whole country, a bit of fun people could understand.' From the first few seconds of their opening comic routine to the final few notes and motions of their closing song and dance, Morecambe and Wise did their very best to draw people together rather than drive them apart. Instead of pandering submissively to the smug exclusivity of the *cognoscenti* (they were flattered when a well-regarded critic praised the sly 'oeillade' that accompanied Eric's sarcastic asides, but they still mocked him mercilessly for his use of the word), and instead of settling – as so many of their supposed successors would do with unseemly haste – for the easy security of a 'cult following', Morecambe and Wise always aimed to entertain the whole nation.

31 The writer implies in the first paragraph that one reason why the show on 25 December 1977 was extraordinary was that

  A light entertainment programmes had been the targets of criticism before then.

  B no one had thought that a British television programme could appeal to all classes.

  C its audience included people who might not have been expected to watch it.

  D people tuning into it knew that they were taking part in a phenomenal event.

32 In the second paragraph, the writer implies that Morecambe and Wise

  A would probably not have been successful had they been solo performers.

  B had a different relationship in real life from the one they had on television.

  C were keen for audiences to realize how professional they were.

  D probably did not know how popular they were.

33 The writer says in the third paragraph that one reason why *The Morecambe & Wise Show* remained so popular was that

  A it adapted to changes in audience attitudes to what constituted good entertainment.

  B it appealed to people who normally preferred other kinds of programme.

  C the people who made it knew that its popularity was guaranteed.

  D the contribution of people other than its stars was a key element in it.

34 The writer suspects that *The Morecambe & Wise Show* will in the future be regarded as

  A something which might only catch on with certain audiences.

  B something which has acquired an exaggerated reputation.

  C the kind of programme that programme-makers will aspire to.

  D the kind of programme that illustrates the disadvantages of technological advances.

35 According to the writer, one feature of *The Morecambe & Wise Show* was

  A the way in which it reflected developments in British society.

  B its inclusion of jokes that only certain people would understand.

  C the consistent way in which other stars were treated on it.

  D its careful choice of other stars to appear on it.

36 In the last paragraph, the writer implies that

  A other comedians have attempted to appeal to only a particular group of people.

  B Morecambe and Wise usually disregarded what critics said about them.

  C other comedians have not accorded Morecambe and Wise the respect they deserve.

  D Morecambe and Wise realized that there were some people who would never like them.

PART 6

You are going to read an extract from a novel. Seven paragraphs have been removed from the extract. Choose from the paragraphs A–H the one which fits each gap (37–43). There is one extra paragraph which you do not need to use. Mark your answers on the separate answer sheet.

AT THE ZOO

Inspector John Rebus was pretending to stare at the meerkats when he saw the man. For the best part of an hour, Rebus had been trying to blink away a headache, which was about as much exercise as he could sustain. He'd planted himself on benches and against walls, wiping his brow even though Edinburgh's early spring was a blood relative of midwinter. His shirt was damp against his back, uncomfortably tight every time he rose to his feet.

37

He hadn't been to the zoo in years; thought probably the last time had been when he'd brought his daughter to see Palango the gorilla. Sammy had been so young, he'd carried her on his shoulders without feeling the strain.

38

Not very, he hoped. The penguin parade had come and gone while he was by the meerkats. Now, oddly, it was when the visitors moved on, seeking excitement, that the first of the meerkats appeared, rising on its hind legs, body narrow and wavering, scouting the territory.

39

There were worse, he had reminded himself, applying his thoughts to the day's central question: who was poisoning the zoo animals of Edinburgh? The fact of the matter was, some individual was to blame. Somebody cruel and calculating and so far missed by surveillance cameras and keepers alike.

40

Meantime, as senior staff had indicated, the irony was that the poisoner had actually been good for business. There'd been no copycat offences yet, but Rebus wondered how long that would last.

The next announcement concerned feeding the sea lions. Rebus had sauntered past their pool earlier, thinking it not overly large for a family of three. The meerkat den was surrounded by children now, and the meerkats themselves had disappeared, leaving Rebus strangely pleased to have been accorded their company.

41

As a child, his roll-call of pets had seen more than its fair share of those listed 'Missing in Action' or 'Killed in the Line of Duty'. His tortoise had absconded, despite having its owner's name painted on its shell; several budgies had failed to reach maturity; and ill-health had plagued his only goldfish. Living as he did in a tenement flat, he'd never been tempted in adulthood by the thought of a cat or dog. He'd tried horse-riding once, rubbing his inside legs raw in the process and vowing afterwards that the closest he'd come in future to the noble beast would be on a betting slip.

42

Except the animals wouldn't share a human's curiosity. They would be unmoved by any display of agility or tenderness, would fail to comprehend that some game was being played. Animals would not build zoos, would have no need of them. Rebus was wondering why humans needed them. The place suddenly became ridiculous to him, a chunk of prime Edinburgh real estate given over to the unreal ... And then he saw the camera.

Saw it because it replaced the face that should have been there. The man was standing on a grassy slope sixty feet away, adjusting the focus on a telescopic lens. His hair was thinning and brown, forehead wrinkled. Recognition came as soon as he lowered the camera.

43

Rebus knew the man. Hadn't seen him in probably four years but couldn't forget eyes like that. Rebus sought for a name, at the same time reaching into his pocket for his radio. The photographer caught the movement, eyes turning to match Rebus's gaze. Recognition worked both ways. And then the man was off, walking briskly downhill. Rebus yanked out his radio.

A He moved away from it, but not too far, and proceeded to untie and tie a shoelace, which was his way of marking the quarter-hours. Zoos and the like had never held any fascination for him.

B Rebus looked away, turning in the direction of its subjects: children. Children leaning into the meerkat enclosure. All you could see were shoe-soles and legs, and the backs of skirts and T-shirts and jerseys.

C Past a restaurant and cafeteria, past couples holding hands and children attacking ice-creams. Peccaries, otters, pelicans. It was all downhill, for which Rebus was thankful. The walkway narrowed just at the point where the crowd thickened. Rebus wasn't sure what was causing the bottleneck, then heard cheers and applause.

D Two more then followed it, appearing from their burrow, circling, noses to the ground. They paid little attention to the silent figure seated on the low wall of their enclosure; passed him time and again as they explored the same orbit of hard-packed earth, jumping back only when he lifted a handkerchief to his face. He was feeling the effects of an early-morning double espresso from one of the kiosks near The Meadows. He'd been on his way to work, on his way to learning that today's assignment was zoo patrol.

E The capybara had looked at him almost with pity, and there had seemed a glint of recognition and empathy behind the long-lashed eye of the hunched white rhino, standing so still it might have been a feature in a shopping mall, yet somehow dignified in its very isolation. Rebus felt isolated, and about as dignified as a chimpanzee.

F Police had a vague description, and spot-checks were being made of visitors' bags and coat pockets, but what everyone really wanted – except perhaps the media – was to have someone in custody, preferably with the tainted tidbits locked away as evidence.

G On the other hand, he'd liked the meerkats, for a mixture of reasons: the resonance of their name; the low comedy of their rituals; their instinct for self-preservation. Kids were dangling over the wall now, legs kicking in the air. Rebus imagined a role reversal – cages filled with children, peered at by passing animals as they capered and squealed, loving the attention.

H Today, though, he had nothing with him but a concealed radio and set of handcuffs. He wondered how conspicuous he looked, walking such a narrow ambit while shunning the attractions further up and down the slope, stopping now and then at the kiosk to buy a can of Irn-Bru.

PART 7

You are going to read an extract from an article about jewellery designers. For questions 44–53, choose from the sections (A–D). The sections may be chosen more than once. Mark your answers on the separate answer sheet.

In which section are the following mentioned?

found that she was launching her jewellery at exactly the tight time? 44 [ ]

is keen for others to focus on what her jewellery represents? 45 [ ]

mentions acting on comments made by others? 46 [ ]

mentions being regarded as an important person? 47 [ ]

does not profit from everything she makes? 48 [ ]

regards her jewellery as having long-term appeal? 49 [ ]

produces pieces that give information on the source of the material used? 50 [ ]

suggests that her jewellery may be too unusual for some people? 51 [ ]

sometimes varies from her usual theme in her jewellery? 52 [ ]

has rejected a certain business method? 53 [ ]

Shining lights: independent jewellery designers

Highly individual jewellery pieces are in demand, and independent designers are putting heart and soul into making them

A Emma Franklin

'It has always been about animals,' Emma Franklin says. 'My friend's grandmother had an amazing stag brooch with huge antlers and that's where it started. Everyone has a relationship with an animal in my collection. When people ask me about an animal I haven't done, I then introduce it to the collection.' Her favourite? 'The ram. It's so strong.' Franklin hand-makes each necklace, bangle, ring, cufflink and pin, featuring any of 14 animal heads, from a pig to a triceratops. All her pieces are made in solid silver, plated in 22ct yellow gold or black rhodium, with black diamonds and freshwater pearls. Bespoke commissions, predominantly engagement rings, not all animal-related, are becoming more frequent. Her clients are all ages, women and men with a bold sense of style. Franklin's robust designs are instantly recognisable, as she has discovered. 'I see a surprising number of people wearing my designs in the street, mainly in east London,' she says. 'Recently in a pub this girl was wearing one of my rings at the bar so I introduced myself. She was completely star-struck and fetched over her dad, who had bought it for her. I had to explain that it was really me who was excited.'

B Alexandra Jefford

'My design style constantly evolves,' Alexandra Jefford says. 'It started out as a throwback to the 1940s, but even though I try new things I can't kick my art background. I'm really inspired by art, architecture, design, furniture design.' Jefford graduated with a degree in fine art, began designing jewellery and sold her first piece, a gold ring, on its first outing, at dinner with a friend. Her designs, produced on a project-by-project basis rather than as collections, include her signature Alphabet series for which she designed a slim font. Her recent O project interprets that letter in various typefaces. Jefford also makes one-off high-end pieces that are more sculptural. Fans range from her daughter's friends to her mother's friends, although she doesn't always want to sell. 'I become emotionally involved with all my pieces so I find it really hard to let go. There are some pieces that I hide "for the family museum". My husband says that I work as a shopper rather than a seller.'

C Hattie Rickards

Hattie Rickards' first collection of 12 rings, entitled Revealed, was an instant success. Her second, Geo, a collection of 15 tactile, geometric necklaces, bracelets, rings, earrings and a brooch, came out to even greater acclaim. 'The ethos behind Geo is connection and relationships, bringing tessellating or geometrical shapes together making one, for example the Kindred ring where two puzzle pieces fit neatly together.' Rickards graduated in jewellery design, then worked for Solange Azagury-Partridge, helping to launch her Madison Avenue store in New York, before setting up on her own. 'I wanted to create a high-end, luxury jewellery brand with an ethical backbone, which coincided with a gap in the market.' All Hattie Rickards Jewellery is made using Fairtrade precious stones from Thailand and India and 18ct Fairtrade, fair-mined gold from Colombia. HRJ is one of the first 20 companies to become a certified user of this type of gold, many of its pieces having the premium 'ecological' label, which ensures no cyanide is used during extraction, which is harmful to the environment. There are no plans for e-commerce, as Rickards believes this detracts from the meaning behind the piece. 'I am passionate that people understand the symbolism behind my work. I don't want it to just be a ring on a website. The story is so important.'

D Mawi Keivom

Mawi Keivom is known for her architectural statement jewellery: chunky box chains with coloured pearls, spiked gold rings and brightly coloured gems. Born in the north-east of India, 40 miles from the Burmese border, into the Mahr tribe, Keivom draws her influences from a peripatetic childhood with her diplomat parents that took them to Africa, the Middle East, south-east Asia and Europe. 'I come from a tribal background and having that heritage has influenced me greatly; the colours, the chunky jewels, the sparkle.' Keivom designs two collections a year. 'My style of jewellery is very individual and not for the faint-hearted. I have a very strong vision that translates into an industrial, graphic aesthetic offset with crystals and pearls that are a little bit feminine. I don't try to do something that is for the moment. My pieces are classics in their own right, not trend-specific.'

WRITING   1 hour 30 minutes

PART 1

Read the two texts below.

Write an essay summarising and evaluating the key points from both texts. Use your own words throughout as far as possible, and include your own ideas in your answer.

Write your answer in 240–280 words.

1

Children's games: past v present

It is characteristic of the human race that change is constantly deplored, and that 'the good old days' are believed to have been far better than the present day. In the realm of children's games, the fixed idea is that children 'don't play games any more', or 'don't have the fun we used to have'. Adults can be savagely critical of the supposed sophistication or inertia of contemporary schoolchildren, and equally self-righteous about their own childhoods. The much re-iterated phrase is, 'We used to make our own amusements.' At the same time, they all but prevent their children from making their own amusements by supplying them with generous pocket-money and giving them expensive toys.

Changes in children's games

If children played their games invariably in the way the previous generation played them, the study of youthful recreation could be a matter merely of antiquarian scholarship. But they do not. Despite the motherly influence of tradition, children's play is like every other social activity; it is subject to continual change. The fact that games are played slightly differently in different places, and may even vary in name, is itself evidence that mutation takes place. And for reasons that are usually social or environmental, some games become impracticable, while others are overlaid or replaced by new versions that are found to be more satisfactory.

Write your essay.

PART 2

Write an answer to one of the questions 2–5 in this part. Write your answer in 280–320 words in an appropriate style.

2   You have recently become aware of the existence of a situation which you believe to be wrong or unjust and which you think should be dealt with by the authorities. Write a letter to a newspaper clearly describing that situation, explaining the problems it causes and saying what you believe should be done about it.

Write your **letter.**

3   Your manager has realized that the staff in your department are unhappy at work at the moment and asked you to write a report on the matter. Write your report, listing the causes of their dissatisfaction, providing examples to illustrate them and explaining what the staff would like to be done to rectify them.

Write your **report.**

4   A magazine has been running a series of articles under the title *Pursuing a Dream* in which successful people describe how they achieved their ambitions and the risks they had to take to do so. The magazine has now invited readers to contribute articles with the same title and you decide to write one. Write your article, describing an ambition you have or had, the risks that you had to take or would have to take in order to achieve it and your attitude to taking risks in general.

Write your **article.**

5   Set book questions – a choice from three questions.

NOTE: There is a sample answer for Question 4 and an assessment of it on page 128.

LISTENING approx. 40 minutes

PART 1

You will hear three different extracts.
For questions 1–6, choose the answer (A, B or C) which fits best according to what you hear.
There are two questions for each extract.

Extract One
You hear a student talking about her experience of doing voluntary work in the Transkei region of South Africa.

1 What does she say about living at 'grass-root' level?
  A Some volunteers found it more difficult to do so than others.
  B The terms of her employment meant that she had no option but to do so.
  C She had not expected to have to do so for the entire year.

2 What does she imply about the culture of the Transkei?
  A There were elements of it she would have preferred not to adopt.
  B It has taught her more than any other experience in her life.
  C There were aspects of it that she did not get fully involved with.

Extract Two
You hear an actor talking about his work as part of a theatre group for children.

3 What does he say about performing on adventure playgrounds?
  A The actors have to keep moving to different parts of them while performing.
  B Children respond more willingly there than in schools.
  C Children keep leaving and coming back while the actors are performing there.

4 Why do the actors 'unmask' at the end of a performance?
  A because the noisier children often demand that they do so
  B in case some of the children have become frightened by them
  C so that the children will start behaving in their usual way again

Extract Three
You hear a man talking about friendship.

5 What does he say about boyhood friendships?
  A Men get a distorted view of what they were really like.
  B There is nothing else to interfere with them.
  C They are the most likely ones to endure for a long time.

6 What does he say about adult friendships?
  A They change in nature according to your circumstances.
  B They can sometimes cause inconvenience.
  C They do not conform with his idea of what real friendship is.

PART 2

You will hear part of a radio programme about the arts.
For questions 7–15, complete the sentences with a word or short phrase.

Some people might describe the home as a [**7**] .

Visitors to the Gallery Ezra can buy [**8**] by Johnny Morris and friends.

Johnny's flatmate said that he should have a [**9**] .

Phoebe Tate and Gareth Harris have given their gallery the name [**10**] .

Phoebe was formerly an [**11**] .

Phoebe and Gareth have been forced to display notices with [**12**] on them.

Visitors to Norman and Valerie Illingworth's cinema sit in seats that are covered in [**13**] .

Some of their cinema's equipment is in what used to be the [**14**] .

The Illingworths have called their cinema [**15**] .

*You will hear an interview with a sports writer about football referees. For questions 16–20,
choose the answer (A, B, C or D) which fits best according to what you hear.*

16 Martin says that referees become concerned if

    A they are no longer chosen for important matches.

    B they cease to cause strong reactions.

    C they feel that other referees do not regard them highly.

    D they attract a lot of attention from strangers.

17 Martin says that referees think they gain the respect of players by

    A resorting to strict discipline when it is necessary.

    B adopting different approaches with different players.

    C showing that they do not care what players think of them.

    D treating players with a certain amount of tolerance.

18 According to Martin, it would be wrong to believe that referees

    A are not passionately interested in football.

    B do not feel that they are performing a duty.

    C are largely motivated by their own vanity.

    D are poorly paid for their efforts.

19 What does Martin say about the system for assessing referees?

    A It causes some referees to be indecisive.

    B It requires referees not to be sensitive people.

    C It enables poor referees to be identified quickly.

    D It leads to inconsistencies in referees' decisions.

20 Martin says that a referee should deal with the bad behaviour of players by

    A informing them that they cannot influence his decisions.

    B admitting to them when he has made a mistake under pressure.

    C deciding rapidly what a player's real intention was.

    D treating the worst offences with the greatest severity.

PART 4

You will hear five short extracts in which people are talking about something currently in the news.
You will hear the recording twice.
While you listen, you must complete both tasks.

TASK ONE

For questions 21–25, choose from the list (A–H) what the news story concerns.

TASK TWO

For questions 26–30, choose from the list (A–H) each speaker's attitude towards the news story.

While you listen, you must complete both tasks.

A a social issue	A scepticism
B a scandal	B amusement
C a crime	C disinterest
D an official announcement	D anger
E a political development	E enthusiasm
F a financial matter	F calmness
G a celebrity	G curiosity
H a health issue	H alarm

Speaker 1		21	Speaker 1	26
Speaker 2		22	Speaker 2	27
Speaker 3		23	Speaker 3	28
Speaker 4		24	Speaker 4	29
Speaker 5		25	Speaker 5	30

SPEAKING 16 minutes

Note: Assessment criteria are on page 93.

PART 2 (4 minutes)

Relaxation

PART 1 (2 minutes)

Questions that may be addressed to either candidate.

- Where are you from?
- Are you working or studying at the moment?
- What hobbies and pastimes do you have?
- How much time do you spend on your hobbies / pastimes?
- Are there any hobbies / pastimes you would like to take up? (Why?)
- What hobbies / pastimes do you find particularly unappealing? (Why?)
- How interested are you in keeping up with news and current affairs?
- Where do you get your information about news and current affairs from?
- Describe something in the news recently which you think was very good.

PART 2 (4 minutes)   Relaxation

(Pictures are on page 64)

For both candidates

Here is a picture of someone relaxing.Talk together about how much opportunity different people have to relax in this way.
(Candidates A and B: 1 minute)

Now look at all the pictures.

Imagine that you are involved in producing a leaflet about how to combat stress and the best way of relaxing.

Talk together about different ways of relaxing. Then decide whether you would use this picture to illustrate the best way of relaxing or whether you would recommend a different way of relaxing.
(Candidates A and B: 3 minutes)

TEST 3

CAMBRIDGE ENGLISH: PROFICIENCY PRACTICE TESTS SPEAKING   65

Task (a)

Candidate A (2 minutes)	**How can a sense of humour be useful to you in life?** ■ dealing with difficult situations ■ in social / working relationships ■ reacting to failure / disappointment
Candidate B (1 minute)	■ Describe a time when your sense of humour has been particularly useful. ■ Describe a time when your sense of humour has got you into trouble. ■ What kind of sense of humour do you share with your friends and / or family? *Candidate A: Do you agree?/What do you think?/How about you?*

Task (b)

Candidate B (2 minutes)	**What aspects of life should always be taken seriously?** ■ family and friends ■ work / education ■ health
Candidate A (1 minute)	■ What do you regard as something that everyone should take seriously? (Why?) ■ Is there something that you regret not having taken seriously? (Why?) ■ What steps do / should you take to look after your health? *Candidate A: Do you agree?/What do you think?/How about you?*

Discussion

■ Describe in general terms the sense of humour in your country.
■ Are there stereotypes in jokes in your country?
■ Is it possible for different cultures to find each other's humour funny? (Why? / Why not?)
■ What kind of humour do people disapprove of in your country? (Why?)
■ What kind of things make you laugh?
■ What subject(s) do you think should never be joked about? (Why?)

(Candidate A and B: 4 minutes)

READING & USE OF ENGLISH   1 hour 30 minutes

PART 1

For questions 1–8, read the text below and decide which answer (A, B, C or D) best fits each gap. Mark your answers on the separate answer sheet.

There is an example at the beginning (0).

Example:

0   A take   **B** put   **C** turn   **D** set

0	A	B	C	D

Marketing Movies

Hyping, or to **0** ____B____ it more politely, marketing movies can double their budget. And in the end, does it really **1** _____ the trick? Those without the major studios' huge spending **2** _____ are not convinced. 'There will always be an audience that follows the big campaigns,' says Andrea Klein, of the British Film Institute, 'but there is another which doesn't **3** _____ to four-page colour ads.' For this audience, reviews are all-important. Publicist Jonathan Rutter concurs: 'Most of our films can be killed **4** _____ dead by bad reviews,' he says.

Although he is not **5** _____ to the odd gimmick, he warns against too much hype: 'I get put off films which are over-marketed,' he says. 'People don't like to be spoon-fed, they prefer to make up their own minds.' For Hollywood blockbusters, **6** _____ people to make up their own minds is not a viable marketing strategy. Films on this scale are caught up in a **7** _____ circle. To **8** _____ inflated production costs a mass audience must be found, and to find that audience takes a giant publicity budget.

1	**A** pull	**B** work	**C** play	**D** do
2	**A** force	**B** strength	**C** weight	**D** power
3	**A** rise	**B** trigger	**C** respond	**D** stir
4	**A** stone	**B** flat	**C** point	**D** cold
5	**A** reluctant	**B** counter	**C** averse	**D** obstinate
6	**A** leaving	**B** availing	**C** consenting	**D** giving
7	**A** relentless	**B** vicious	**C** brutal	**D** merciless
8	**A** restore	**B** refund	**C** recover	**D** reimburse

PART 2

For questions 9–16, read the text below and think of the word which best fits each gap. Use only one word in each gap. There is an example at the beginning (0). Write your answers IN CAPITAL LETTERS on the separate answer sheet.

Example:

0	I	N												

THE KARAOKE CULTURE

We live in a culture that values participation over ability: the karaoke culture. **0** _In_ broadcasting, it seems we cannot escape the vogue for 'access TV', 'people shows' and 'video diaries'. **9**_____ is our apparent obsession with documenting our own lives that, in future, programmes will be replaced by cameras in every room, so that we can watch **10**_____ endlessly on TV. In the countless shows that fill our daytime schedules, **11**_____ audience has become the star. The public make programmes, the public participate in programmes, the public become performers. Anybody **12**_____ do it!

But there is a world of difference between enjoying something and joining in. If we all join in, **13**_____ is the point of artists or experts? If everything is accessible, **14**_____ can be no mystery, no mystique. I love listening to a genius and learning from (or even just appreciating) his or her skill. **15**_____ assume then that I can 'have a go at' their craft **16**_____ be monstrous impudence on my part.

For questions **17–24**, read the text below. Use the word given in capitals at the end of some of the lines to form a word that fits in the gap in the same line. There is an example at the beginning (**0**). Write your answers **IN CAPITAL LETTERS on the separate answer sheet**.

Example:

0	T	R	A	I	N	E	E					

TEST 4

BUSINESS PRESENTATIONS

Ancient man used sticks of charcoal to draw pictures on cave walls in order to
communicate (with, probably, their deities and **0** _trainee_ huntsmen).   **TRAIN**
Today, their direct **17** _____ are required to demonstrate that they can   **DESCEND**
use much more sophisticated tools with **18** _____ in order to make   **EASY**
effective presentations to today's business audiences. In a business environment
in which the presentation of clear, easily understandable information is a
19 _____ and in which memorability is key, managers should be constantly   **NECESSARY**
20 _____ their equipment to keep pace with developments.   **GRADE**

Audiences expect high-quality presentations that are **21** _____ stimulating **VISION**
and get the message across without wasting time. Professionally made
presentations clearly **22** _____ that the person giving them has thought   **SIGNIFICANT**
through the issues and knows what they are talking about. They can put a
23 _____ case that wins over an audience and they can put you, or your   **PERSUADE**
your company, in the most **24** _____ light possible.   **ADVANTAGE**

PART 4

For questions 25–30, complete the second sentence so that it has a similar meaning to the first sentence, using the word given. **Do not change the word given.** *You must use between three and eight words, including the word given. Here is an example (0):*

Example:

0 Dan definitely won't be able to afford a holiday this year.

possiblity

There _____ to afford a holiday this year.

0	is no possibility of Dan being able

Write **only the missing words on the separate answer sheet.**

---

25 Once I made sure there was no reason to be afraid, I went ahead.

fear

Having satisfied _____ , I went ahead.

26 The manager praised one particular player.

singled

One particular player _____ praise by the manager.

27 He denied the accusation unconvincingly, which made me think he was guilty.

led

His _____ believe that he was guilty.

28 There came a time when I completely ran out of patience.

stage

I _____ more patience left.

29 It is likely that she will get very angry when she finds out.

liable

She _____ fit when she finds out.

30 Being inexperienced was a disadvantage to her when she applied for promotion.

counted

Her _____ when she applied for promotion.

PART 5

Fat Mikey

Even in my dewy days, I never gazed at the world wide-eyed with wonder. If I wasn't born shrewd, at least I grew up too smart to be naive. So how come in the prime of my life, at the height of my powers, I could not foresee what would happen in the Torkelson case? Was I too street smart? Had I been around the block so many times that I had finally lost my sense of direction?

Ages ago, soon after I became a criminal defense lawyer, Fat Mikey LoTriglio hailed me across the vast concrete expanse of the courthouse steps. 'Hey, girlie!' His tomato of a face wore an expression that seemed (I squinted) amiable, pretty surprising considering he'd just been sprung from Elmira after doing two and a half years on the three counts of aggravated assault I'd prosecuted him for.

'Come over here,' he called out. 'Hey, I'm not going to kill you.' In Fat Mikey's world, that was not hyperbole but a promise; he got busy straightening his tie to demonstrate he was not concealing a Walther PPK. 'I hear you're not working for the D.A. any more,' he boomed. I strolled over, smiling to show I didn't hold any grudges either, and offered my hand, which he shook in the overly vigorous manner of a man trying to show a professional woman that he's comfortable with professional women. Then I handed him my business card. I was not unaware that Fat Mikey was one of three organized crime figures the cops routinely picked up for questioning on matters of Mob-related mayhem. To have Fat Mikey as a client was to have an annuity.

He glanced down at my card to recall my name. 'Lee?'

Naturally, I didn't respond 'Fat?' And to call him 'Mike' after having called him 'a vulture feasting on society's entrails' in my summation might seem presumptuous. So I murmured a polite 'Mmm?'

'A girl like you from a good family –'

'Are you kidding?' I started to say, but he wouldn't let me.

'I could tell you got class, watching you at the trial,' he went on. 'You know how? Good posture – and not just in the morning. Plus you say 'whom.' Anyways, you really think you can make a living defending guys like me?' He didn't seem so much sexist as sincerely curious. 'This is what you had in mind when you went to law school?' he inquired.

'No. Back then I was leaning toward Eskimo fishing rights. But this is what I'm good at.'

He shook his head at my folly. 'When a guy's ass is in a sling, you think he's gonna hire a girl who says 'whom'?'

'If he's partial to his ass he will.'

Fat Mikey's upper lip twitched. For him, that was a smile. Then, almost paternally, he shook a beefy index finger at me. 'A girl like you should be more particular about the company she keeps.'

Years later, I would learn how wise Fat Mikey was.

Nevertheless, from the beginning I knew there were limits to keeping bad company. I could be sympathetic to my clients without getting emotionally involved. A lot of them had had sad childhoods. Many had been victims of grievous social injustice, or of terrible parents (who were themselves victims of terrible parents). Still, I never forgot they were criminals. And while I may have delighted in a bad guy's black humour, or a tough broad's cynicism, I was never one of those attorneys who got naughty thrills socializing with hoods. You'd never catch me inviting a client – let's say Melody Ann Toth, for argument's sake – to go shopping and out for meals so we could chitchat about old beaux ... or about what she might expect at her upcoming trial for robbing three branches of the Long Island Savings Bank on what might have been an otherwise boring Thursday.

For their part, most of my clients (including Fat Mikey, who retained me two years after that conversation on the courthouse steps) wouldn't think I was exactly a laugh a minute either. Whatever their personal definition of a good time was, I wasn't it. Unlike me, Fat Mikey simply did not get a kick out of crocheting afghans or listening to National Public Radio. With fists the size of rump roasts, Mikey looked like what he was: a man for whom aggravated assault was not just a profession but a pleasure. As for Melody Ann, with her pink-blonde hair that resembled attic insulation, the only reason she'd go shopping at Saks would be to knock off the Estée Lauder counter when she ran out of lip liner. My clients had no reason or desire to try to pass for upper middle class.

For that reason alone, Norman Torkelson was different right from the beginning.

31 When Fat Mikey shouted 'Hey, girlie!', the narrator

    A had a brief feeling of guilt about what she had previously done to him.

    B had difficulty in distinguishing what sort of mood he was in.

    C thought that it was impossible for him to be out of prison already.

    D remembered that he had been given a shorter prison sentence than expected.

32 The narrator gave Fat Mikey her business card because

    A she felt that he could be of advantage to her in her present job.

    B she felt that it would show that there was no bad feeling between them.

    C she wanted to behave in a way she thought appropriate for professional women.

    D she feared that there was a danger of him becoming aggressive.

33 What do we learn about Fat Mikey's trial?

    A The narrator's use of 'whom' during it had struck Mikey as being inappropriate.

    B Mikey felt that her contribution at it had been crucial to the outcome.

    C The narrator's description of him at it made it hard for her to treat him like a friend.

    D Mikey felt that her behaviour at it had been inappropriate for a woman.

34 When they talked about her suitability as a defender,

    A Mikey said that he did not think she would do well when defending certain people.

    B the narrator was puzzled as to what he meant by the advice he gave her.

    C Mikey felt that his comments on the subject might have offended her.

    D the narrator said that people who wanted to get out of trouble would employ her.

35 What does the narrator imply about some other attorneys?

    A They attracted criticism because of their relationships with some of their clients.

    B They paid too much attention to the unfortunate backgrounds of some of their clients.

    C They became friendly with some of their clients despite knowing that they shouldn't.

    D They weren't as interested in some of their clients as they pretended to be.

36 What does the narrator say about the majority of her clients?

    A Their personal appearance was important to them.

    B They committed crimes they were not likely to get away with.

    C They regarded her as something of a disappointment.

    D It would not occur to them to socialize with her.

PART 6

You are going to read an article. Seven paragraphs have been removed from the article. Choose from the paragraphs A–H the one which fits each gap (37–43). There is one extra paragraph which you do not need to use. Mark your answers **on the separate answer sheet.**

HELP GUIDE US THROUGH THE UNIVERSE

Sir Martin Rees, Astronomer Royal, launches this year's Young Science Writer competition

If you ask scientists what they're doing, the answer won't be 'Finding the origin of the universe', 'Seeking the cure for cancer' or suchlike. It will involve something very specialised, a small piece of the jigsaw that builds up the big picture.

37

So, unless they are cranks or geniuses, scientists don't shoot directly for a grand goal – they focus on bite-sized problems that seem timely and tractable. But this strategy (though prudent) carries an occupational risk: they may forget they're wearing blinkers and fail to see their own work in its proper perspective.

38

I would personally derive far less satisfaction from my research if it interested only a few other academics. But presenting one's work to non-specialists isn't easy. We scientists often do it badly, although the experience helps us to see our work in a broader context. Journalists can do it better, and their efforts can put a key discovery in perspective, converting an arcane paper published in an obscure journal into a tale that can inspire others.

39

On such occasions, people often raise general concerns about the way science is going and the impact it may have; they wonder whether taxpayers get value for money from the research they support. More intellectual audiences wonder about the basic nature of science: how objective can we be? And how creative? Is science genuinely a progressive enterprise? What are its limits and are we anywhere near them? It is hard to explain, in simple language,

even a scientific concept that you understand well. My own (not always effective) attempts have deepened my respect for science reporters, who have to assimilate quickly, with a looming deadline, a topic they may be quite unfamiliar with.

40

It's unusual for science to earn newspaper headlines. Coverage that has to be restricted to crisp newsworthy breakthroughs in any case distorts the way science develops. Scientific advances are usually gradual and cumulative, and better suited to feature articles, or documentaries – or even books, for which the latent demand is surprisingly strong. For example, millions bought *A Brief History of Time*, which caught the public imagination.

41

Nevertheless, serious books do find a ready market. That's the good news for anyone who wants to enter this competition. But books on pyramidology, visitations by aliens, and suchlike do even better: a symptom of a fascination with the paranormal and 'New Age' concepts. It is depressing that these are often featured uncritically in the media, distracting attention from more genuine advances.

42

Most scientists are quite ordinary, and their lives unremarkable. But occasionally they exemplify the link between genius and madness; these 'eccentrics' are more enticing biographees.

43

There seems, gratifyingly, to be no single 'formula' for science writing – many themes are still under-exploited. Turning out even 700 words seems a daunting task if you're faced with a clean sheet of paper or a blank screen, but less so if you have done enough reading and interviewing on a subject to become inspired. For research students who enter the competition, science (and how you do it) is probably more interesting than personal autobiography. But if, in later life, you become both brilliant and crazy, you can hope that someone else writes a best-seller about you.

A However, over-sensational claims are a hazard for them. Some researchers themselves 'hype up' new discoveries to attract press interest. Maybe it matters little what people believe about Darwinism or cosmology. But we should be more concerned that misleading or over-confident claims on any topic of practical import don't gain wide currency. Hopes of miracle cures can be raised; risks can be either exaggerated, or else glossed over for commercial pressures. Science popularisers – perhaps even those who enter this competition – have to be as sceptical of some scientific claims as journalists routinely are of politicians.

B Despite this, there's a tendency in recent science writing to be chatty, laced with gossip and biographical detail. But are scientists as interesting as their science? The lives of Albert Einstein and Richard Feyman are of interest, but is that true of the routine practitioner?

C Two mathematicians have been treated as such in recent books: Paul Erdos, the obsessive itinerant Hungarian (who described himself as 'a machine for turning coffee into theorems') and John Nash, a pioneer of game theory, who resurfaced in his sixties, after 30 years of insanity, to receive a Nobel prize.

D For example, the American physicist Robert Wilson spent months carrying out meticulous measurements with a microwave antenna which eventually revealed the 'afterglow of creation' – the 'echo' of the Big Bang with which our universe began. Wilson was one of the rare scientists with the luck and talent to make a really great discovery, but afterwards he acknowledged that its importance didn't sink in until he read a 'popular' description of it in the *New York Times*.

E More surprising was the commercial success of Sir Roger Penrose's *The Emperor's New Mind*. This is a fascinating romp through Penrose's eclectic enthusiasms – enjoyable and enlightening. But it was a surprising best seller, as much of it is heavy going. The sales pitch 'great scientist says mind is more than a mere machine' was plainly alluring. Many who bought it must have got a nasty surprise when they opened it.

F But if they have judged right, it won't be a trivial problem – indeed it will be the most difficult that they are likely to make progress on. The great zoologist Sir Peter Medawar famously described scientific work as 'the art of the soluble'. 'Scientists,' he wrote, 'get no credit for failing to solve a problem beyond their capacities. They earn at best the kindly contempt reserved for utopian politicians.'

G This may be because, for non-specialists, it is tricky to demarcate well-based ideas from flaky speculation. But it's crucially important not to blur this distinction when writing articles for a general readership. Otherwise credulous readers may take too much on trust, whereas hard-nosed sceptics may reject all scientific claims, without appreciating that some have firm empirical support.

H Such a possibility is one reason why this competition to encourage young people to take up science writing is so important and why I am helping to launch it today. Another is that popular science writing can address wider issues. When I give talks about astronomy and cosmology, the questions that interest people most are the truly 'fundamental' ones that I can't answer: 'Is there life in space?', 'Is the universe infinite?' or 'Why didn't the Big Bang happen sooner?'

You are going to read an extract from an article about the Greek philosopher Socrates. For questions 44–53, choose from the sections (A–D). The sections may be chosen more than once. Mark your answers on the separate answer sheet.

In which section are the following mentioned?

relationships between people in Socrates' time	**44**
the continuing importance of Socrates' beliefs	**45**
the writer's theory concerning what happened to Socrates	**46**
why little is known about Socrates as a man	**47**
how the writer set about getting information relevant to Socrates	**48**
the difference between common perceptions of Socrates and what he was really like	**49**
an aim that Socrates was critical of	**50**
the realization that finding out about Socrates was a difficult task	**51**
how well known Socrates was during his time	**52**
an issue that Socrates considered in great detail	**53**

Seeking Socrates

It may be more than 2,400 years since his death, but the Greek philosopher can still teach us a thing or two about leading 'the good life'. Bettany Hughes digs deeper.

A Sharing breakfast with an award-winning author in an Edinburgh hotel a few years back, the conversation came round to what I was writing next. 'A book on Socrates,' I mumbled through my muesli. 'Socrates!' he exclaimed. 'What a brilliant doughnut subject. Really rich and succulent with a great hole in the middle where the central character should be.' I felt my smile fade because, of course, he was right. Socrates, the Greek philosopher, might be one of the most famous thinkers of all time, but, as far as we know, he wrote not a single word down. Born in Athens in 469BC, condemned to death by a democratic Athenian court in 399BC, Socrates philosophized freely for close on half a century. Then he was found guilty of corrupting the young and of disrespecting the city's traditional gods. His punishment? Lethal hemlock poison in a small prison cell. We don't have Socrates' personal archive; and we don't even know where he was buried. So, for many, he has come to seem aloof and nebulous – a daunting intellectual figure – always just out of reach.

B But that is a crying shame. Put simply, we think the way we do because Socrates thought the way he did. His famous aphorism, 'the unexamined life is not worth living', is a central tenet for modern times. His philosophies – 24 centuries old – are also remarkably relevant today. Socrates was acutely aware of the dangers of excess and overindulgence. He berated his peers for a selfish pursuit of material gain. He questioned the value of going to fight under an ideological banner of 'democracy'. What is the point of city walls, warships and glittering statues, he asked, if we are not happy? The pursuit of happiness is one of the political pillars of the West. We are entering what has been described as 'an age of empathy'. So Socrates' forensic, practical investigation of how to lead 'the good life' is more illuminating, more necessary than ever.

C Rather than being some kind of remote, tunic-clad beardy who wandered around classical columns, Socrates was a man of the streets. The philosopher tore through Athens like a tornado, drinking, partying, sweating in the gym as hard as, if not harder than the next man. For him, philosophy was essential to human life. His mission: to find the best way to live on earth. As Cicero, the Roman author, perceptively put it: 'Socrates brought philosophy down from the skies.' And so to try to put him back on to the streets he loved and where his philosophy belonged, I have spent 10 years investigating the eastern Mediterranean landscape to find clues of his life and the 'Golden Age of Athens'. Using the latest archaeology, newly discovered historical sources, and the accounts of his key followers, Plato and Xenophon, I have endeavoured to create a Socrates-shaped space, in the glittering city of 500BC Athens – ready for the philosopher to inhabit.

D The street jargon used to describe the Athens of Socrates' day gives us a sense of its character. His hometown was known as 'sleek', 'oily', 'violet-crowned', 'busybody' Athens. Lead curse tablets left in drains, scribbled down by those in the world's first true democracy, show that however progressive fifth-century Athenians were, their radical political experiment – allowing the demos (the people) to have kratos (power) – did not do away with personal rivalries and grudges. Far from it. In fact, in the city where every full citizen was a potent politician, backbiting and cliquery came to take on epic proportions. By the time of his death, Socrates was caught up in this crossfire.

E His life story is a reminder that the word 'democracy' is not a magic wand. It does not automatically vaporize all ills. This was Socrates' beef, too – a society can only be good not because of the powerful words it bandies around, but thanks to the moral backbone of each and every individual within it. But Athenians became greedy, they overreached themselves, and lived to see their city walls torn down by their Spartan enemies, and their radical democracy democratically voted out of existence. The city state needed someone to blame. High-profile, maddening, eccentric, freethinking, free-speaking Socrates was a good target. Socrates seems to me to be democracy's scapegoat. He was condemned because, in fragile times, anxious political masses want certainties – not the eternal questions that Socrates asked of the world around him.

WRITING 1 hour 30 minutes

PART 1

Read the two texts below.

Write an essay summarising and evaluating the key points from both texts. Use your own words throughout as far as possible, and include your own ideas in your answer.

Write your answer in 240–280 words.

1

Fundamental questions about human nature

There can be no single, simple definition of human nature. Many inter-twining ideas in the history of philosophy have helped us to form our understanding of ourselves. Ideas of human nature radically affect the kind of society we live in and the kind we would like to live in. How far do we need society? Is it feasible to imagine living in splendid isolation? Linked to this is the question as to whether we are all naturally only concerned for ourselves, and only willing to cooperate with others when it is in our interests to do so. Are we, on the other hand, social beings by nature, eager to cooperate with others for the common good?

The study of human nature

Ideas about human nature are of their essence philosophical. They are not simply the result of scientifically established facts, but are general conceptions arrived at through rational argument. They are inevitably often controversial, but the theories produced determine our vision of ourselves. Most writing on the subject is explicitly philosophical. Since, though, philosophical assumptions about our nature lie at the root of any discipline concerned with the activities of men and women, it is not surprising that some thinkers have written primarily from the standpoint of another intellectual discipline. History, politics and social anthropology, to name only the most obvious, all proceed with some view about human nature.

Write your essay.

PART 2

Write an answer to one of the questions 2–5 in this part. Write your answer in 280–320 words in an appropriate style.

---

2   A magazine is running a competition for the most interesting review of a tourist attraction. Write a review, describing the attraction you have chosen and commenting on why it is worth visiting or why you would not recommend it to other people.

Write your **review.**

3   You have read a newspaper article about young people today, in which the writer criticizes today's youth for spending their time watching TV and playing computer games rather than reading books or going out and doing sport. The newspaper's editor has asked readers to respond to the article. Write a letter to the newspaper addressing the points made in the article and giving your own views.

Write your **letter.**

4   A local newspaper is planning to publish a series of articles by readers under the title *Local Hero* and you decide to send in an article for the series. Write your article, describing the local person you have chosen and explaining why you believe that person is worthy of recognition.

Write your **article.**

5   Set book questions – a choice from three questions.

NOTE: There is a sample answer for Question 3 and an assessment of it on page 129.

LISTENING approx. 40 minutes

PART 1

You will hear three different extracts.
For questions 1–6, choose the answer (A, B or C) which fits best according to what you hear.
There are two questions for each extract.

Extract One
You hear the start of a radio programme about the National Dragonfly Museum in Britain.

1 We are told that one of the aims of the museum is to
   A emphasize how attractive dragonflies are.
   B take action to affect the fate of dragonflies.
   C investigate the problems dragonflies face.

2 The speaker suggests that dragonflies
   A have moods similar to those of human beings.
   B are aware of the fact that people are watching them.
   C are more aggressive than is generally known.

Extract Two
You hear part of a radio programme about an American boy who invented a popular toy.

3 What does the presenter imply about the Water Talkie?
   A Some people may suspect that it was not really Richie's idea.
   B It is the sort of toy that an adult would never think of.
   C It has made Richie more money than he should have at his age.

4 What do we learn about the development of the Water Talkie?
   A Toy retailers were unhappy with its appearance at first.
   B A fundamental problem with it took a long time to solve.
   C It might not have been possible but for Richie's grandfather.

Extract Three
You hear a writer talking about a cookbook she has written.

5 What does she say about her own book?
   A It takes into account the way people really live their lives.
   B It is written in a style usually associated with fiction.
   C It has fewer illustrations than other cookbooks.

6 She says that so many cookbooks are published because people
   A use them as a substitute for actually cooking.
   B are starting to care more about their personal lives than their careers.
   C are too lazy to come up with their own ideas for cooking.

PART 2

You will hear part of a talk about shopping centres.
For questions 7–15, complete the sentences with a word or short phrase.

David says that people building shopping centres need to concentrate on what he refers to as

[_____ **7**] .

He has discovered that women don't like it if there are a lot of [_____ **8**]
on their journey to a shopping centre.

For the floors of shopping centres, [_____ **9**] are not acceptable.

People consider that shopping centres with a lot of [_____ *and* _____ **10**] in them
are better than others.

David has come up with the term [_____ **11**] to describe shoppers who
have a lot in common with each other.

In the shopping centre he has most recently been involved with, there are
[_____ *and* _____ **12**] malls.

David calls shoppers who are no longer ambitious in life [_____ **13**] .

David calls shoppers who haven't got much money and are looking for bargains
[_____ **14**] .

For David, newly married couples may come into the category of
[_____ **15**] .

You will hear part of a radio phone-in programme about journalists who interview famous people. For questions 16–20, choose the answer (A, B, C or D) which fits best according to what you hear.

16 In his introduction, the presenter says that celebrity interviewers

    A attract more attention than they probably wish to.

    B are pleased to be regarded as possessing great expertise.

    C are given considerable prominence in most British papers.

    D require different skills from other types of journalist.

17 Lynn Barber says that her approach involves

    A pointing out contradictions in what interviewees have said previously.

    B asking only questions that interviewees will have difficulty answering.

    C making it clear that she does not believe some of what interviewees tell her.

    D making interviewees who she dislikes believe that she likes them.

18 What does Zoe Heller say about the people she interviews?

    A She is glad that they do not have an opportunity to interview her.

    B Few of them appreciate how much effort she puts into her interviews.

    C She is less concerned about upsetting some of them than others.

    D They should not be surprised by what happens when she interviews them.

19 Angela Lambert dislikes it when interviewees

    A ask her to leave out minor matters.

    B think that she genuinely likes them a lot.

    C accuse her of insincerity.

    D are too nervous to speak openly.

20 Ray Connolly implies that his approach may involve

    A making sure that interviewees stick to the order he has decided on.

    B trying to make interviewees sound more interesting than they really are.

    C rephrasing things interviewees say if they don't make sense.

    D excluding comments that interviewees may come to regret.

PART 4

You will hear five short extracts in which people are talking about people they know.
You will hear the recording twice.
While you listen, you must complete both tasks.

TASK ONE

For questions **21–25**, choose from the list (**A–H**) what each speaker says is a good characteristic of the person.

While you listen, you must complete both tasks.

A	generosity
B	loyalty
C	sense of humour
D	perception
E	willingness to adapt
F	honesty
G	confidence
H	drive to succeed

Speaker 1		**21**
Speaker 2		**22**
Speaker 3		**23**
Speaker 4		**24**
Speaker 5		**25**

TASK TWO

For questions **26–30**, choose from the list (**A–H**) what each speaker regards as a bad characteristic of the person.

A	secretive
B	jealous
C	narrow-minded
D	unsympathetic
E	rude
F	introverted
G	childish
H	unreliable

Speaker 1		**26**
Speaker 2		**27**
Speaker 3		**28**
Speaker 4		**29**
Speaker 5		**30**

SPEAKING 16 minutes

Note: Assessment criteria are on page 93.

PART 2 (4 minutes)

Travel

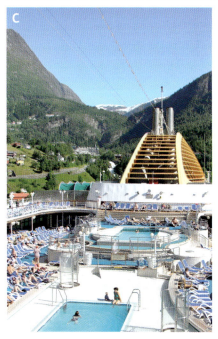

PART 1 (2 minutes)

Questions that may be addressed to either candidate.

- Where are you from?
- Are you working or studying at the moment?
- What career plans do you have?
- When did / will you decide on the career you are going to have?
- How ambitious are you?
- What do you think is the best aspect of life in your country?
- What do you think is the worst aspect of life in your country?
- What place in your country would you most recommend to a visitor?
- What are the main interests of people of your age in your country?

PART 2 (4 minutes)   Travel

(Pictures are on page 84)

For both candidates

Here are some pictures of people travelling. Look at pictures D and E and talk together about the advantages and disadvantages of travelling in these ways.
(Candidates A and B: 1 minute)

Now look at all the pictures.

Imagine that you are involved in producing a short film about travel experiences that young people today find appealing. These pictures show different travel experiences that the film might focus on.

Talk together about what is appealing about the different ways of travelling shown in the pictures. Then decide which way of travelling the film should focus on as the most appealing to young people today.
(Candidates A and B: 3 minutes)

TEST 4

Task (a)

Candidate A (2 minutes)	**How important is it for people to do creative things?** ■ most common forms of creativity ■ what benefits people get from creative activities ■ fitting creative activities in with work / study
Candidate B (1 minute)	■ What creative thing that you have done has brought you the greatest satisfaction? ■ Is there something creative that you would like to be able to do but can't? ■ Have you been encouraged to be creative? *Candidate A: Do you agree?/What do you think?/How about you?*

Task (b)

Candidate B (2 minutes)	**In what ways is it important to be practical in life?** ■ practical skills required in everyday life ■ society's need for people in practical jobs ■ disadvantages of lacking practical skills
Candidate A (1 minute)	■ Would you describe yourself as practical or creative or both? ■ How did you learn the practical skills that you have? ■ Is there something practical that you would like to be able to do but can't? *Candidate A: Do you agree?/What do you think?/How about you?*

Discussion

■ Can people learn to be creative or does it have to come naturally?
■ Is too much or too little importance given to creativity in the modern world?
■ How common is it for people to be able to make a living from creative activities?
■ What practical skills should everyone have?
■ Why do some people have more practical skills in everyday life than others?
■ What are the disadvantages of not having practical skills in everyday life?

(Candidate A and B: 4 minutes)

 **UNIVERSITY** *of* **CAMBRIDGE**
ESOL Examinations

Do not write in this box

Candidate Name
If not already printed, write name
in CAPITALS and complete the
Candidate No. grid (in pencil).

Candidate Signature

Examination Title

Centre

Supervisor:

If the candidate is ABSENT or has WITHDRAWN shade here ⬜

Centre No.

Candidate No.

**Examination
Details**

0	0	0	0
1	1	1	1
2	2	2	2
3	3	3	3
4	4	4	4
5	5	5	5
6	6	6	6
7	7	7	7
8	8	8	8
9	9	9	9

Candidate Answer Sheet 1

Instructions

Use a PENCIL (B or HB). Rub out any answer you wish to change using an eraser.

Part 1: Mark ONE letter for each question.

For example, if you think **B** is the right
answer to the question, mark your
answer sheet like this:

Parts 2, 3 and **4:** Write your answer clearly
in CAPITAL LETTERS.

For Parts 2 and 3 write one letter
in each box. For example:

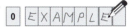

Part 1

1	A	B	C	D
2	A	B	C	D
3	A	B	C	D
4	A	B	C	D
5	A	B	C	D
6	A	B	C	D
7	A	B	C	D
8	A	B	C	D

Part 2

Do not write
below here

9		9 1 0 u
10		10 1 0 u
11		11 1 0 u
12		12 1 0 u
13		13 1 0 u
14		14 1 0 u
15		15 1 0 u
16		16 1 0 u

Continues over ➡

CPE R1

DP690/190

Part 3

		Do not write below here
17		17 1 0 u
18		18 1 0 u
19		19 1 0 u
20		20 1 0 u
21		21 1 0 u
22		22 1 0 u
23		23 1 0 u
24		24 1 0 u

SAMPLE

Part 4

		Do not write below here
25		25 2 1 0 u
26		26 2 1 0 u
27		27 2 1 0 u
28		28 2 1 0 u
29		29 2 1 0 u
30		30 2 1 0 u

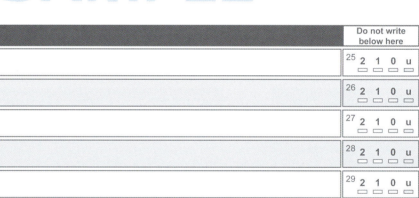

denote Print Limited 0121 520 5100

PHOTOCOPIABLE

UNIVERSITY *of* **CAMBRIDGE**
ESOL Examinations

Do not write in this box

Candidate Name
If not already printed, write name
in CAPITALS and complete the
Candidate No. grid (in pencil).

Candidate Signature

Examination Title

Centre

Supervisor:

If the candidate is ABSENT or has WITHDRAWN shade here

Centre No.

Candidate No.

Examination
Details

Candidate Answer Sheet 2

Instructions
Use a PENCIL (B or HB). Rub out any answer you wish to change using an eraser.
Parts 5, 6 and 7: Mark ONE letter for each question. For example, if you think **B** is the right answer to
the question, mark your answer sheet like this:

| 0 | A | B | C | D |

Part 5

31	A	B	C	D
32	A	B	C	D
33	A	B	C	D
34	A	B	C	D
35	A	B	C	D
36	A	B	C	D

Part 6

37	A	B	C	D	E	F	G	H
38	A	B	C	D	E	F	G	H
39	A	B	C	D	E	F	G	H
40	A	B	C	D	E	F	G	H
41	A	B	C	D	E	F	G	H
42	A	B	C	D	E	F	G	H
43	A	B	C	D	E	F	G	H

Part 7

44	A	B	C	D	E	F
45	A	B	C	D	E	F
46	A	B	C	D	E	F
47	A	B	C	D	E	F
48	A	B	C	D	E	F
49	A	B	C	D	E	F
50	A	B	C	D	E	F
51	A	B	C	D	E	F
52	A	B	C	D	E	F
53	A	B	C	D	E	F

CPE R2

denote Print Limited 0121 520 5100

DP691/191

UNIVERSITY *of* **CAMBRIDGE**
ESOL Examinations

Do not write in this box

Candidate Name
If not already printed, write name in CAPITALS and complete the Candidate No. grid (in pencil).

Candidate Signature

Examination Title

Centre

Supervisor:

If the candidate is ABSENT or has WITHDRAWN shade here ▭

Test version: A B C D E F J K L M N

Special arrangements: S H

Centre No.

Candidate No.

Examination Details

0	0	0	0
1	1	1	1
2	2	2	2
3	3	3	3
4	4	4	4
5	5	5	5
6	6	6	6
7	7	7	7
8	8	8	8
9	9	9	9

Candidate Answer Sheet

SAMPLE

Instructions

Use a PENCIL (B or HB).
Rub out any answer you wish to change using an eraser.

Parts 1, 3 and **4:**
Mark ONE letter for each question.

For example, if you think **B** is the right answer to the question, mark your answer sheet like this:

Part 2:
Write your answer clearly in CAPITAL LETTERS.

Write one letter or number in each box.
If the answer has more than one word, leave one box empty between words.

For example:

Turn this sheet over to start.

CPE L

DP692/192

PHOTOCOPIABLE

Part 1

	A	B	C
1			
2			
3			
4			
5			
6			

Part 2 (Remember to write in CAPITAL LETTERS or numbers)

Do not write below here

7		7 1 0 u
8		8 1 0 u
9		9 1 0 u
10		10 1 0 u
11		11 1 0 u
12		12 1 0 u
13		13 1 0 u
14		14 1 0 u
15		15 1 0 u

SAMPLE

Part 3

	A	B	C	D
16				
17				
18				
19				
20				

Part 4

	A	B	C	D	E	F	G	H
21								
22								
23								
24								
25								
26								
27								
28								
29								
30								

denote Print Limited 0121 520 5100

Assessing the Writing Paper

The Writing Paper tasks are marked from 0 to 5 according to four subscales:

- Content
- Communicative Achievement
- Organization
- Language

Content is common to all levels, while separate descriptors are referred to for each level for Communicative Achievement, Organization, and Language.

CONTENT

This focuses on how well the task has been fulfilled, in other words if candidates have done what the task asks them to do.

ORGANIZATION

This focuses on how well the answer has been constructed, and if it is logical and well-structured.

COMMUNICATIVE ACHIEVEMENT

This focuses on the appropriacy of writing for the task, including the correct register.

LANGUAGE

This focuses on vocabulary and grammar, including accuracy as well as range of language.

Answers which are longer than the guidelines given on length may include content irrelevant to the task, and may have a negative effect on the reader; answers which are too short may not include all the information required and may not display an adequate range of language. These could affect the marks on the relevant subscales. Answers should use a consistent variety of English in areas such as spelling and should not therefore switch between American and British English words or spellings.

Assessing the Speaking Paper

Assessment is based on performance in the whole test, and is not related to performance in particular parts of the test. Students are assessed on their own performance, and not in relation to each other.

Marks are awarded by the assessor, who does not take part in the test, according to five analytical criteria: *Grammatical Resource, Lexical Resource, Discourse Management, Pronunciation*, and *Interactive Communication*. The interlocutor, who conducts the test, gives a mark for *Global Achievement*.

GRAMMATICAL RESOURCE

This refers to a candidate's ability to maintain control fo a wide range of grammatical forms. At Cambridge English: Proficiency level candidates can also show a level of flexibility of use.

LEXICAL RESOURCE

This refers to a candidate's ability to use a range of appropriate vocabulary with flexibility in order to give and exchange views on familiar, unfamiliar and abstract topics.

DISCOURSE MANAGEMENT

This refers to the extent, relevance, coherence and cohesion of a candidate's individual contributions. At Cambridge English: Proficiency level, candidates can produce extended and shorter stretches of language, as required by the task, with very little hesitation and using a wide range of cohesive devices and discourse markers. Contributions must be relevant, coherent and varied.

PRONUNCIATION

This refers to the intelligibility of a candidate's speech. First language interference is expected and not penalised if it does not have a negative effect on the listener. At Cambridge English: Proficiency level, candidates are expected to have control of phonological features, i.e. intonation, word and sentence stress, and the articulation of individual sounds.

INTERACTIVE COMMUNICATION

This refers to a candidate's ability to use language to achieve meaningful communication through initiating, responding, exchanging information and developing the interaction. At Cambridge English: Proficiency level, candidates are expected to interact with ease, linking contributions to those of other speakers, to widen the scope of the interaction and to negotiate towards an outcome.

TEST 1

Reading & Use of English

1 **B** If someone **sweeps someone off their feet**, they cause the other person to fall in love with them as soon as they first meet them.

   A If someone **plucks** someone from a place, they rescue them when they are in a dangerous or unpleasant situation.

   C If someone **drags their feet**, they deliberately respond slowly to something because they do not want it to happen quickly, or at all.

   D If you **hoist** someone or something, you physically lift them to a higher position.

2 **A** **Without so much as** = without even. The writer is saying that her cousin's wife rudely ignored the writer when she arrived, acting as if the writer wasn't there.

   B **As/So far as** = to the extent that, e.g. in expressions like 'As/So far as I know'.

   C The structure **so + adjective/adverb + as to do** = to such an extent that something results ('Don't work so hard as to make yourself ill').

   D **As/So long as** = only if ('I'll lend it to you as long as you promise to give it back later').

3 **A** If someone **proceeds to do** something, they do it after completing another action.

   B If someone **follows one action with another**, or **by doing** something, they complete one action and then do another.

   C If someone **progresses to a certain level or stage**, they move to that level or stage after completing a previous one.

   D If someone **continues to do/doing something**, they do the same action for a period of time, they do not stop doing it.

4 **B** If you **glare at** someone, you look at them with an angry expression on your face.

   A If you **wink at** someone, you give a private and friendly signal to someone by looking at them and then closing and opening one eye very quickly.

   C If you **peep at** something, you look at it quickly and secretly, especially through a small opening.

   D If you **eye** someone or something, you look at them because you are interested in, attracted to, or suspicious of them.

5 **D** If you **deem** someone/something (to be) something, you consider them to be that thing or your judgement is that they are that thing. The writer is saying that her cousin's wife only decided to pay attention to the writer when the writer paid the bill for the meal – she became pleasant at the

time when the writer was doing something for her.

   A If you **ponder (on)** something, you think about it carefully and for a long time in order to reach a decision or form an opinion.

   B If you **discriminate between** people or things, you distinguish between them so that you regard them differently from each other rather than considering them to be all the same.

   C If you **weigh (up)** something, you think about the negative and positive aspects of it before reaching a decision. If you **weigh someone up**, you watch them and their behaviour carefully in order to form an opinion of them.

6 **D** If something **serves someone's purpose**, it enables them to achieve an aim, or is suitable in terms of their own wishes. The writer is saying that her cousin's wife was only nice to people when she felt that this would benefit her in some way.

   A If someone or something **meets** a requirement, a need, a demand, etc., they satisfy or fulfil it.

   B If you **realize** an ambition, you achieve it or make it happen.

   C If someone or something **performs** a task, they carry it out or do it.

7 **D** **Truly** = really, genuinely, rather than only appearing to be or pretending to be.

   A **Fully** = completely, in every way.

   B **Purely** = no more than, simply, only.

   C **Literally** = really, factually, even though it may be surprising.

8 **C** If something **depends on something else**, it is completely affected or influenced by it or changes because of it.

   A If something **varies according to** something, it changes because of the influence of something

   B If something **revolves around** something, it has it as its main or only influence or aspect.

   D If something **is determined by** something, it is completely affected by or influenced by it ('an attitude to life determined by childhood experiences').

9 **known**

If someone is *known to someone as something*, they are called that thing or given that name by that person.

10 **did**

The structure *do nothing + infinitive* is used for emphasis with the meaning 'certainly not do'.

11 **made**

The structure *make + object + adjective* = 'cause + object + to be + adjective'.

12 to

If someone is *given to something/doing something*, they tend to do or experience something considered undesirable.

13 among

The phrase *among + a group of people* is used when talking about something shared by or common to people in that group.

14 out

If you point out that something *is the case*, you say that it is the case because others may not have noticed that it is, or you draw attention to the fact that it is the case.

15 called

If someone calls someone *something*, they describe them as being that thing or say that they belong to a certain category.

16 what

The writer is saying that Schulz had to ask what the meaning of the word 'existentialist' was, because although someone said Schulz was an existentialist, he wasn't familiar with the word himself. This follows from the point about him not being an intellectual and therefore not knowing things such as philosophical terms.

PART 3 1 MARK PER QUESTION (TOTAL 8)

17 belies

If something *belies something*, it creates a false impression because it conceals something significant that contrasts with how it appears.

18 rehearsal

A *rehearsal* is an occasion when people practise performing something that they are going to perform in public.

19 insight

If you *get/gain an insight into something*, you learn something about the true nature of it.

20 chilly

This means 'cold' or 'rather cold'.

21 memorable

If something is *memorable*, it creates a powerful impression, with the result that it is remembered for a long time afterwards.

22 authenticity

This means 'the quality of being genuine rather than specially created but intended to appear genuine'.

23 teamwork

This means 'a group of people working in cooperation with each other to achieve a common aim'.

24 indicative

If something is *indicative of something*, it shows, suggests or gives an idea of it.

PART 4 2 MARKS PER QUESTION (TOTAL 12)

25 dropped/given a hint (1 mark)
that he no longer (1 mark)

If someone *drops/gives a hint* that something is the case, they say something that suggests indirectly that it is the case. In this phrase 'hint' is a noun; in the first sentence it is a verb.

The structure *subject + no longer + verb* = subject + negative verb + any longer.

26 were five actors (1 mark)
in contention for (1 mark)

In this sentence *There* acts as the subject instead of 'Five actors' in the first sentence and it is therefore immediately followed by the verb 'were' and 'five actors' to form the structure *there + to be + noun*.

If someone is *in contention for something*, they are one of a group who are all competing for and trying to get it and who all have at least some chance of getting it.

27 so wrapped up (1 mark)
in her work (1 mark)

In this sentence, *wrapped up* acts as an adjective in the structure *so + adjective + that*, which replaces the structure *so + adverb + that* in the first sentence.

If you are *wrapped up in something*, you are concentrating very hard on it or are completely absorbed or involved in it, so that it has all your attention and you do not notice other things.

28 to find out (1 mark)
what the cause of (1 mark)

The structure *yet + infinitive* means 'not done yet/ still not done but perhaps will be done'. The structure *subject + still + negative auxiliary + past participle* in the first sentence has to be replaced by the structure *subject + positive auxiliary + yet + infinitive*.

In the second part of the sentence, the verb 'caused' has to be changed to the noun *cause*, which is followed by the preposition of.

29 (some) reluctance that (1 mark)
I put/wrote my signature (1 mark)

In this sentence the adverb has to be changed to the structure *with + noun* and the noun from 'reluctantly' is 'reluctance'.

If you *put your signature on/to something*, you sign it with your name.

30 to technical knowledge (1 mark)
I'm/I am no match (1 mark)

The phrase *when it comes to something/doing something* means 'when the situation is a matter of/ relates to' or 'when the subject is'.

If *someone/something is no match for someone/ something*, they are not at all equal to the other thing/person because they are very inferior to them.

ANSWER KEY

PART 5 2 MARKS PER QUESTION (TOTAL 12)

31 D The writer says that the pictures are *brutally exact* (accurate in a way that could be considered cruel) in the sense that they *reproduce every detail of a style of life* (the use of the indefinite article 'a' here means that the writer is referring to one of many different styles of life that exist). He is therefore saying that they show accurately a particular lifestyle, the lifestyle of some people who live in cities. He then lists some of the features of that lifestyle (the kind of cigarette-lighter such people use, the kind of jewellery they wear and what they have in their homes), his point being that these things are shown in the pictures in advertisements.

32 A The writer says that the images *radically conflict with each other* and that if you *swap* (exchange) *the details about between the pictures, they are instantly made illegible* (impossible to read) – an image in one advertisement would not look appropriate in another. He then says that the characters shown in advertisements are so different from each other that none of them has *an individual claim to speak for society as a whole*, and lists the different kinds of character shown in advertisements. He then says that these characters *provide a glossy mirror of the aspirations* (hopes, desires, ambitions) *of a representative city crowd*. His point therefore is that these images reflect what typical city dwellers want to be like, but that city dwellers themselves consist of different kinds of people with different aspirations.

33 D The writer says that the portraits of previous generations of movie stars had a *degree of romantic unparticularity* (romantic images that were all similar to each other), *as if they were communal dream projections of society at large* (representations of the fantasies of society in general) and that the only exceptions to this were the portraits of movie stars who were known for their appearances in certain specific kinds of film – *westerns* (films about cowboys in the Wild West), *farces* (comedy films based on ridiculous misunderstandings) *and gangster movies* (films about criminal gangs). These stars, he says, had *odd* (strange), *knobbly* (with bumps rather than smooth) *cadaverous* (pale and thin) *faces* and they played characters who fitted into the category of *the hero as loner* (main characters who operated alone rather than with others). Such characters *belonged to history or the underworld* (the criminal part of society), lived on *the perimeter*

(edge) of society and reminded people of society's *dangerous edges*. His point therefore is that most portraits of movie stars showed romantic figures and the exceptions were those who reminded people that there were some dangerous elements in society, although these were only on the edge of society. He is therefore implying that most people at that time thought that they lived in a pleasant society in which they were safe and in which people who were dangerous were exceptions.

34 B The writer says that the voices of stars of the last decade are *strenuously* (involving a lot of effort) *idiosyncratic* (individual, different from others and perhaps strange) and that *whines* (high-pitched and unpleasant and annoying continuous sounds), *stammers* (speech impediments involving long pauses and frequently repeated beginnings of words because the person cannot speak properly) *and low rumbles* (deep, low, continuous sounds) *are exploited* (used to the maximum advantage) *as features of 'star quality'* (the qualities a person has that are considered the reasons why they have become or could become a star). He is therefore saying that they consciously try to speak in these ways, which are not pleasant to listen to or easy to hear, in order to sound different from any other actor, and that the fact that their voices have a sound that is individual to them is part of what gives them 'star quality'.

35 A The writer says that it is possible to see when looking at a crowd on an underground platform a *honey-comb* (a complex thing full of small compartments) *fully-worked-out* (formed in every detail after careful thought) *worlds, each private, exclusive, bearing little comparison with its nearest neighbour*. The writer says that in a city *the isolate* (individual who keeps apart from everyone else) *and the eccentric* (strange but harmless) *push to the centre of the stage* (put themselves into a position in which others pay attention to them) and that such people *have as good a claim to the limelight* (the focus of attention) *and the future as anyone else*. His point therefore is that you can see on an underground platform all kinds of different people, each of whom has different characteristics and different attitudes to life and that each of these sees themselves as having as much importance or value as anyone else. Everyone is an individual, he is saying, and no one has much in common with anyone else.

36 C The writer says that a new arrival in a city realizes that *there are so many people he might become* and that if he buys certain things, this will *go* some way (make some progress) *towards turning him into a personage* (a person with distinct characteristics) *even before he discovers who that personage is.* In other words, new arrivals can start to get a certain image as a result of what they buy, before they have been living in the city long enough to know what the sort of people who have that image are really like.

PART 6 2 MARKS PER QUESTION (TOTAL 12)

37 E
In E, the first word *This* refers to the experience the writer had had during his initial interview, and he says that this experience was *a foretaste* (an example in advance) of Eilbeck's favourite method of floating an idea (suggesting an idea for consideration). In the paragraph after the gap, *these brainstorms* refers back to the discussions and the ideas exemplified in E.

38 H
In the first sentence of H, *so well* means 'as well as the idea described in the paragraph before the gap'. In the paragraph after the gap, the writer says that, fortunately for him, Eilbeck didn't tell him to write any of the stories that were based on his *extemporized* (invented without previous thought) headlines.

39 C
At the beginning of C, *This* refers back to *some small task* in the paragraph before the gap. The writer gives an example of such a task – writing a short article about some ghosted showbiz memoirs (the autobiography of someone in the world of entertainment that is in fact written by someone else). He then describes an occasion when Eilbeck told him to write such an article. After the gap, the writer goes on to describe another of *my little chores* (tasks) – another *small task* in addition to the one just described in C.

40 F
At the beginning of F, *This* refers back to the writer's task of rewriting part of the astrology column, mentioned in the paragraph before the gap. He says that he was told to do this because one of the paper's executives was *a passionate believer in it* – *it* here refers to astrology. In the first sentence of the paragraph after the gap, *he* refers to the executive mentioned in F.

41 G
In G, the writer moves on to introduce a new subject, that of his month's trial coming to an end. In the paragraph after the gap, he gives an example of an occasion when he really did have the chance to write something. *For example* immediately after the gap, refers back to what he says at the end of G about some opportunities not being false alarms.

42 B
In the first sentence of B, *this commission* refers back to the task of being in charge of a new gossip column that is mentioned in the paragraph before the gap. In the paragraph after the gap, the writer says that he was lucky in that he was given someone to *hold my hand* (help him) in this *insane* (crazy) *exercise* (activity) – this phrase refers back to the task of producing a gossip column according to Eilbeck's instructions, as mentioned in B.

43 D
In the first sentence of D, *the deadline* refers to the time by which the gossip column had to be ready for publication and the writer says that this was looming. This follows from his description in the paragraph before the gap of the way they produced the column and the difficulty they had in producing it. In the final paragraph, the writer says that the gossip column *itself* ground to a halt – the use of *itself* here means that not only did their enterprise (talking to servants) end but so did the whole column. The phrases *came to a stop* and *ground to a halt* have the same general meaning and are used to say that both things came to an end.

PART 7 1 MARK PER QUESTION (TOTAL 10)

44 C The writer says that in Valrhona's newest factory, there are *paintings of the chefs who are fans of Valrhona.*

45 D Pierre Costet believes that assumptions about the three kinds of cacao bean are *exaggerated*. What is *widely accepted* and *considered* is in fact *too simplistic*, according to him.

46 B When Valrhona first introduced a 70 per cent cocoa solids chocolate bar, it *caused a flurry* (a big reaction) *among chefs*, who used it in their dishes and gave it *star billing on menus* (named it as the most important ingredient).

47 A The recipes in Valrhona's book are *mesmerizingly complex creations strictly for trained chefs or time-rich amateurs* – they are too complicated for people who are not trained chefs or ordinary people with a lot of time to spend on them.

48 B The contrast is between *boutique chocolate makers*, who carry out the whole process of creating chocolate themselves, turning beans into chocolate bars, and the *many other companies* who buy ready-made chocolate and then form it into bars and other products.

49 C They bought modern machines for their factory and they were much more efficient. However, they *just didn't produce such good chocolate*, and so the company decided to return to using the old machines, from the 1960s.

50 A The writer explains the term 'tempering', which is one stage in the preparation of chocolate. It is one of the 'techniques' that is in the book and is explained in the bracketed part of the sentence.

51 C The various ingredients are *ground together to make a paste* and this paste has to contain grains that are no bigger than 17 microns. This is because the grains should not be felt by the tongue.

52 D The writer asks Pierre Costet whether it is possible to use *too much cocoa solids* in a chocolate bar and he says that it is. The flavour of some chocolate might not be what is wanted if the amount of cocoa solids is too great.

53 D Pierre Costet says that *how the beans are grown and fermented* has a big influence on the quality. If Forestero beans are *well looked after*, they can be of a higher quality than Criollo beans that have been *poorly treated*, even though Criollo beans are generally considered to be of a much higher quality than Forestero beans.

Writing

MARK SCHEMES
MARKS OUT OF 20 FOR EACH QUESTION
ASSESSMENT CRITERIA ARE ON PAGE 92.

QUESTION 1

Content
The essay should include a summary of these four key points:

Text 1 (a) damage done to places by tourism
(b) damage done to local people by tourism

Text 2 (a) tourism industry rejects criticism that it does damage
(b) some changes in tourism industry too late or for image only

Communicative Achievement
This is an essay and so the register should be neutral or formal. The reader should be clear both as to what the key points in each text are and the candidate's own opinions and responses to those points.

Organization
The essay should be coherently organized in paragraphs, with clear linking between the summaries of the key points and the candidate's own views. An introduction and conclusion are not essential.

Language
The essay should contain an appropriate level of accurate grammar and vocabulary. Vocabulary connected with the topics of tourism and the environment should be correctly used, as should grammatical structures for describing and comparing points of view/information, presenting and supporting opinions, and linking points in complex sentences.

FOR A SAMPLE ANSWER AND ASSESSMENT OF IT, SEE PAGE 126.

QUESTION 2

Content
Article should describe an historical event from the point of view of someone who was there, giving that person's impressions of what happened.

Communicative Achievement
Register appropriate for a magazine article – could be formal, informal or neutral but should be consistent throughout. Reader would be interested in following the account and would have a clear idea of the impressions events made on the writer.

Organization
Clear development of narration and description, with clear chronology. Appropriate paragraphing and linking between description of events and observations on them. Article format – perhaps sub-headings for paragraphs. Paragraphs may be short for impact.

Language
Language of narration and description.

QUESTION 3

Content
Report should include:
• how research was carried out
• recommendations concerning new facilities and entertainment
• analysis of the benefits that would result

Communicative Achievement
Register appropriate for student making recommendations to someone in authority – formal or neutral. Report should be in sections, with clear section headings. Reader would understand precisely what the writer is proposing, the evidence that has led to what is proposed and the writer's beliefs as to the benefits.

Organization
The report should be well-structured with clear sections, each dealing with separate aspects. Ideas should be presented in a clear, readable way, although note-form may be used where appropriate. There should be appropriate linking within, and perhaps between, sections.

Language
Language of analysis, description (of the facilities and entertainment), narration (how the research was done), hypothesizing and recommending.

QUESTION 4

Content
Review should inform the reader about the programme and evaluate it in terms of whether it merits the popularity it has.

Communicative Achievement

Register should be appropriate for a review in a magazine of this kind – it could be informal (or amusing), fairly formal or neutral. Format should be appropriate for a review, with clear paragraphing. Reader would be informed about the series and why it is popular, and would have a clear idea of the writer's views on it.

Organization

Clear development. combining description of various aspects of the series with comments on those. Appropriate linking between paragraphs and between description and comment within paragraphs.

Language

Language of narration, description and evaluation, including language for expressing and supporting views. Candidates may praise or criticize the series throughout, or combine praise with criticism.
FOR A SAMPLE ANSWER AND ASSESSMENT OF IT, SEE PAGE 126.

Listening

PART 1 1 MARK PER QUESTION (TOTAL 8)

1 **B** The speaker says that nobody knows what the phrase means *beyond the vague idea that* (although they do understand from it that it means that) *the arts and sciences are worryingly separate and at loggerheads* (in direct opposition and total disagreement). The use of the word *worryingly* is crucial here, because by using it the speaker indicates that he regards the situation described as something which does or should cause people to worry.

2 **C** The speaker uses sarcasm (language intended to have the opposite of its real meaning in order to criticize) when talking about Snow. He says that he *distinguished himself* (this normally means 'made himself noticed and admired') not because he worked in both the arts and science but because he achieved nothing in either the field of the arts or the field of science (in other words, he was exceptional because he failed in both fields).

3 **C** The speaker says that all the reasons were genuine, but then gives examples of two categories of reason. She lists reasons such as that the dog ate the tickets, and says that these are *quite apart from* (totally different or separate from) *the ones* (the reasons) *you'd expect*. She is therefore saying that some reasons for losing tickets were predictable and normal but that others were not the sort you'd expect, which means that these others, though also genuine, are harder to believe.

4 **A** In her story, there are two places called Rochester

in different parts of the US and someone at her agency booked the man on a flight to the wrong one. When he got back and went back to the agency, *he saw the funny side of it* (understood that there was an amusing aspect to what happened, rather than thinking it was totally bad, and therefore found it amusing to a certain extent). Because of that he was not *ranting and raving* (shouting angrily and complaining loudly). By saying that he wasn't 'ranting and raving', the speaker is strongly implying that it could have been expected that he would have done that because of the mistake the agency had made, and that it would have been understandable if he had reacted in that way.

5 **B** Victoria says that Freddie is called 'Snakeboy' because *he's always picking them up, and walking about with them round his neck* – nobody would do that unless they liked touching snakes.

6 **C** The reporter says that the place looks *exotic* (extremely attractive and unusual) but that Mark *is quick to dispel any notions of tasting paradise* (keen to deny the idea that they are experiencing life in an ideal place). Mark then lists several unpleasant aspects of their lives there – damage caused by rain, mudslides, lack of a proper water supply, having to go on donkeys to collect water, primitive sleeping accommodation and no privacy. He is therefore making it clear that their lives are not like living in paradise and emphasizing the problems they face in their daily lives.

PART 2 1 MARK PER QUESTION (TOTAL 9)

7 **classified advertising**
She says that she first worked for Business Traveller magazine and that her job there involved selling classified advertising by phone (dealing with people placing and paying for small advertisements in a special section of the magazine).

8 **Soundcraft Electronics**
After three years of doing her first job, she got a job at Soundcraft Electronics as a marketing co-ordinator (person responsible for organising the various aspects of some work so that they all function together well).

9 **film library**
She joined Visnews as a marketing executive in its film library. In this context, a library is a place where documents or old items no longer in use are stored as a record which can be consulted.

10 **documentaries**
She started to work in a new department that made and sold videos; these films were documentaries that had to have *a special-interest theme* (be on a subject of interest to particular people rather than people in

general).

11 direct marketing

She says that the videos were sold *at retail outlets* (in shops) and *through direct marketing techniques* (methods involving selling directly to members of the public rather than through shops, for example mail order).

12 launch event

The deal involved her company using the theme park for *a launch event* (an occasion when a company first shows a new product to potential customers and to people working in the same business) and, in exchange for being allowed to use the theme park for this event, her company put some publicity or an advertisement for the theme park on the front of the video itself.

13 Special Locations Department/operation

She rejoined Visnews and worked in this department as a sales co-ordinator at first, but she says this is *the operation I now head* (am now in charge of).

14 camera crews

She says that her department offers *camera crews* (teams of people working together operating cameras to make films and programmes) as well as *editing facilities*.

15 PR/Public Relations agency

She says that she has a *mentor* (somebody who has a lot of experience of a certain type of work and gives advice to someone with less experience, and is trusted by that person) who worked in a PR agency she had contact with when she first worked at Visnews.

PART 3 1 MARK PER QUESTION (TOTAL 5)

16 B Susan says that *the one thing I do despise* (intensely dislike) *is the politician who tries to have things all ways* (in this context, this means 'hold every opinion that everyone could want them to have, rather than giving a single opinion'). Such a politician, she says, isn't someone who says they haven't made their mind up about something, it is a politician whose attitude is *'actually, I think this'* (this is my actual opinion), but this opinion is unpopular with voters so I'm going to *dress it up* (hide the real nature of it by making it appear different from what it really is) and *present it in a different way to the electorate* (voters). Her point is that she intensely dislikes politicians who make their opinions appear different from what they really are when they are addressing voters, because they know that their real opinions would not be popular with voters.

17 A The interviewer says that the disagreement may have resulted in her political future being *closed off*

(it may have meant the end of her political career). She says that she felt this situation was *the time of trial* for her (a situation in which her qualities as a person and her beliefs were being tested). She says that if she had allowed her own political future *to weigh with me* (influence me, be a very important factor in my decisions) with regard to an issue she regarded as extremely important, *it really wouldn't be worth having as a political future* – she felt there would be no point in her continuing as a politician if her concern for her own career strongly influenced her regarding a very important issue. She says that *to look at self-advancement* (personal progress or success in a career) *in its own right* (as a separate, individual thing), *it isn't worth a damn* (it is of no value at all) – in other words, there is no value in succeeding in your career simply in order to be successful, you should care about other things too. Her point therefore is that the disagreement led her to conclude that she cared more about issues she had strong beliefs about than about becoming more successful as a politician.

18 D She says that, although she agrees with the interviewer that colleagues supported her privately but not publicly, one or two did support her publicly. However, she told them not to because she wanted to act alone in this situation without *embroiling* (involving in a difficult situation) other people. She says that politics doesn't always involve getting other people involved in such situations, and that this was an occasion when it wasn't necessary or desirable. She says that, instead of involving colleagues, she *made my doubts and reservations known* and it was then *up to my colleagues* (it was my colleagues' decision, they could choose) whether or not to take her views into consideration. She therefore didn't ask colleagues to support her, she told them what she thought and let them make up their own minds whether or not they agreed with her.

19 C She says that when you *take a stand on something* (express a strong view on something, resulting in disagreement), your opinion of your colleagues is bound to be *coloured* (influenced) by whether they support you, oppose you or remain neutral. However, she says that politics is *a kaleidoscope* (a constant and quickly changing pattern) *of changing alliances* (situations in which people join together in agreement with each other), and so people you are strongly opposed to on one occasion can be people you are *allied with* (joined with in agreement) on another occasion. She is therefore sure that in the future there will be situations when *some of those colleagues and I will* swap (exchange) positions – instead of them not supporting her, she won't support them. Her point therefore is that because of the nature of politics, in the future there will be times when she does not support the same people who did not support her at that time.

20 **C** She says that she is not at all surprised that some colleagues thought she was *bonkers* (mad, crazy), because there are some politicians who think that *you* (by this she means politicians in general) should never *rock the boat* (do something that causes problems because it upsets the established situation or way of doing things), and should *always put yourself first* (consider your own interests more important than anything else), and she had done the opposite of both those things. She is therefore saying that she was considered mad because she had not conformed with common notions of what politicians should do.

PART 4 1 MARK PER QUESTION (TOTAL 10)

21 **H** The speaker wanted to find out more about the subject, which was the history of the period of time when the speaker was very young. Adults in his family had talked about various matters but he was too young *to engage with it all then*. Now he wants to *find out more about what was going on then*.

22 **G** The speaker bought the book in an airport because she thought it *would pass the journey in an easy enough way* – give her something to do during the flight.

23 **B** The speaker bought the book because he wanted to *break the habit* of not reading 'serious' books.

24 **E** The speaker says that she *got given the book* – it was a present. She only read it because the person who had given it to her might ask her what she thought of it.

25 **C** The speaker wanted to see *what all the fuss was about* – why the book attracted so much praise. He had read reviews which *made big claims for it as a major and important work* and he wanted to find out if the reviews were accurate.

26 **B** The speaker says that the book was *lively* and not at all *dry* (it was entertaining rather than too serious and factual). It *made the events and changes of that period come to life* – it made them seem real and was interesting and enjoyable to read.

27 **D** The speaker says that the story is *very complicated* and that the reader has to *concentrate hard to follow what's going on*. It wasn't a *light read* – something that can be read easily and without much thought, and she had to *keep going back*

to check things – look at earlier parts of the book in order to be clear about what she was reading further on.

28 **H** The speaker says that the book has become a *surprise best-seller* and has a *cult following* (it is loved by a large group of people who are passionate about it).

29 **A** The speaker says that the book isn't good and her doubts about it were accurate. She thinks the book and the writer are given too much praise that they do not deserve and it is *beyond me* (she cannot understand at all) how such a poor book gets published or why it is *critically acclaimed* (praised a lot by critics).

30 **G** The speaker says that the writer presents *some interesting points of view* which *make you question your assumptions and look at the issues from a very different angle*.

TEST 2

Reading & Use of English

PART 1 1 MARK PER QUESTION (TOTAL 8)

1 **Ⓐ** **For want of** = because there is a lack of, because of the absence of. The writer is saying that he cannot think of a better word to describe the third category of books than 'anecdotal' (based on amusing or interesting short accounts of things that happen to people).
  B **In the absence of** = because something does not exist or is not present.
  C If there is **a shortage of** something, there is not as much of it as is required.
  D If there is **a need for** something, it is lacking but necessary.

2 **Ⓑ** If the difference between things is **blurred**, it is difficult to be certain what the difference is because they seem similar in some ways. The writer is saying that it is hard to separate travel books into clearly different categories because they often have the features of more than one category.
  A If a piece of glass, such as a window, someone's glasses or a car windscreen **mists up/over**, it becomes covered in mist so that it is difficult or impossible to see through it.
  C If one thing **blends with** another, for example ingredients in a dish, sounds, colours, etc, it goes together with it to form an effective or attractive mixture.
  D If something, for example a description or some information, is **sketchy**, it is not clear because it

ANSWER KEY

does not have enough detail.

3 **(B)** If you are **loath to do** something, you don't want to do it, you are reluctant to do it. The writer is saying that travel writers do not want to be put into rigid and narrow categories.

  A If you are **wary of** something or someone, you are suspicious of them, do not trust them and feel that they may do you some harm if you are not careful.

  C If you are **cautious about** something, you are careful with regard to it because you do not want to make a mistake or allow it to result in bad consequences.

  D If you are **resistant to** something, you oppose it and try or wish to prevent it from happening.

4 **(B)** A **mixture of** one thing and another is a combination of the two things, something that is formed by the different things.

  A A **merger** is when two or more companies or organizations join together to form one company or organization.

  C If something is **a cross between** two things, it is a mixture of the two things. This would be correct if the sentence said 'a cross between the documentary and the creative'.

  D A **compound** is a substance or chemical that is formed by mixing two or more substances or chemicals together.

5 **(C)** If someone **claims to be** something or claims that something is the case, they say that this is the case but they are not necessarily telling the truth and others may doubt what they say.

  A If you **allege that** something is the case or if something is alleged to be the case, you say that something unpleasant or unacceptable about someone else is the case but do not or cannot prove this.

  B If you **hold** a certain view, you have a certain opinion or belief. If you hold that something is the case, you believe or say that it is the case.

  D If you **contend that** something is the case, you say or argue that it is the case, particularly when others have different views.

6 **(C)** If someone **employs something in order to do something**, they use it for that purpose.

  A If someone **engages with** something, they focus on it and give their attention to it.

  B If someone **exerts influence on** something, they use their influence to affect something.

  D If someone **exercises influence/authority**, they use their influence or authority in order to do something.

7 **(A)** If something **counts**, it matters or is important in terms of a particular situation.

B If you **reckon with** something, you take it into consideration.

C If something **bears on** something, it relates to or affects it.

D If something **signifies** something, it is an indication of it.

8 **(D)** If two things or people **are made for each other**, the two go together perfectly and are completely suited to each other.

  A If someone is **given to something/doing something**, they do it habitually, particularly when such a habit is considered strange or unacceptable.

  B If someone is **cut out for/to do** something, for example a certain kind of work or a certain role in something, they are well suited to it because of the personality, skills, etc. that they have.

  C If something **lends itself** to something, it is suitable for a particular use or purpose, which may not be its original or intended use or purpose.

PART 2 1 MARK PER QUESTION (TOTAL 8)

9 **itself**
If something is *an end in itself*, it is an aim on its own and not because of its connection with anything else.

10 **better**
The structure *the + comparative adjective ... the + comparative adjective ...* is used for talking about two things that are related, with the second being the result of the first.

11 **so**
The linking phrase *so that* links an action or situation with its purpose or result.

12 **anyone/anybody/everyone/everybody**
The writer's point in the next sentence is that it's not difficult to become famous, and here that point is introduced.

13 **been/seemed/appeared**
The structure here, an inversion because the sentence begins with 'Never', is *Never + auxiliary + subject + past participle*. In a simpler way, it could be expressed as 'Fame has never been/seemed/appeared more democratic' but the use of 'Never' at the beginning makes the point more emphatic.

14 **No/Small/Little**
The phrase *No/Small/Little wonder* means 'It is not at all surprising that ... ' The writer is saying that, because of what is stated in the previous sentence, it is not surprising that in the modern age, becoming famous is a common ambition.

15 **the**
The structure *the + adjective* means 'people who are + adjective'.

16 being

If something *rewards someone for something/doing something*, it gives them something good in return for something they have done.

PART 3 1 MARK PER QUESTION (TOTAL 8)

17 breathtaking

If something is *breathtaking*, it is so extraordinary that it surprises or excites someone seeing or experiencing it enormously.

18 settlers

Settlers are the first people to go and live in a certain place when it has been discovered.

19 lifetime

Someone's *lifetime* is the whole of their life. The phrase *the + noun + of a lifetime* means 'a unique or exceptional thing' or 'something that will never happen or be available again'.

20 consistent

In this context, this means 'always there and always the same'. The advert is saying that snow conditions in Colorado never change.

21 legendary

In this context, this means 'extremely well-known' or 'very strongly associated with a person or place'.

22 reality

If something *turns into/becomes (a) reality*, it actually happens or is experienced, rather than remaining something that is only wished for or that is only a possibility.

23 picturesque

This means 'very attractive to look at'. It is most commonly used to describe scenery or buildings in places that people might visit and that they may wish to photograph.

24 unparalleled

If something is *unparalleled*, it has no equal because it is better or worse than any other.

PART 4 2 MARKS PER QUESTION (TOTAL 12)

25 often I see it (1 mark)
I never tire of (1 mark)

The structure *however + adjective/adverb* means 'no matter how/it doesn't matter how/it makes no difference how + adjective/adverb'.
If you *tire of something/doing something*, you stop being interested in or wanting to do it and you begin to find it boring because you have done or experienced it a great many times.

26 what prompted Fred to make (1 mark)
so extraordinary (1 mark)

If something *prompts someone to do something*, it causes them to do it by giving them the idea that they should do it. In this sentence, 'why' has to be changed

to the pronoun 'what' (meaning 'the thing which') to provide a subject for the verb 'prompted'.
The structure *such + a/an + adjective + noun* can also be expressed, more emphatically, by the structure so + adjective + a/an + noun.

27 of efficiency (1 mark)
reflects badly on (1 mark)

The phrase *(a) lack of + uncountable noun* = 'not enough of' or 'complete absence of' something. The negative adjective 'inefficient' has to be changed into the positive noun 'efficiency'.
If something *reflects well/badly on someone/something*, it gives a good/bad impression of them or makes them appear good/bad.

28 with the utmost (1 mark)
care (1 mark)

The phrase *the utmost + uncountable noun* means 'the greatest possible amount of something'.
If something is done *carefully*, it is done with care. The structure *with + noun* is used to describe how something is done.

29 gave him my word (1 mark)
(that) there would be (1 mark)

If you *give someone your word* that something will be the case, you promise them that it will be the case.
In the second part of the sentence, *there* must be used to provide a subject because the subject 'the situation' in the first sentence is not a subject in this sentence. The negative 'would not be' has to be changed to the positive 'would be' because the negative is now supplied by the phrase 'no repetition'.

30 a young musician (1 mark)
Tim modelled himself on (1 mark)

In this context, *As* means 'when he was' and simply replaces that phrase.
If you *model yourself on someone*, you try to copy them or be like them because you admire them or consider that they are a very good example of something you are trying to be.

PART 5 2 MARKS PER QUESTION (TOTAL 12)

31 D Paul saw the baby turtles going across the beach and back into the sea, where the ones who *escaped being flipped over* (turned over quickly) *on their backs and pecked to death* (killed by being bitten) *by wading birds* (birds with long legs that feed in shallow water) *were finally swallowed up in the surf* (waves). That the vast majority did not manage to get into the sea and disappear but were killed is made clear by the fact that we are told that *one or two were bound to slip through unnoticed* (it was inevitable that one or two turtles would get through and disappear away into the sea without the wading birds noticing and killing them), because there were so many baby turtles and the sea was so big that it was inevitable that some would not be killed. We are therefore told that a large number of baby turtles were born but that only 'one or two' were not killed.

32 C Paul felt that if there was a turtle whose *instinct* (natural feeling) *towards multiplication* (reproduced) *was misformed* (not formed in the normal way) or absent, or whose instincts were not to reproduce but to think about the *purpose of reproduction* or to find out how long it could *stay underwater on one breath* (without breathing again), this instinct *would die with the turtle*. Such a turtle, he therefore thought, would be an exception and its instincts would cease to exist when it died because it would be the only turtle to have those instincts.

33 B We are told that parenthood had taken Paul by surprise and that despite all the books and articles he had read on the subject and the classes he had attended to prepare people for it, he had not been ready for *the intensity of it all*. Becoming a parent had therefore been such an intense experience that he just wanted to go to sleep so that he could achieve *the cessation* (ending) *of thought*. If he didn't want to think any more, this must have been because he was mentally exhausted as a result of all the thoughts he had had on becoming a parent.

34 B He felt that *something had obliged him to* (made him feel he must) *seek out* (find) *a tranquil* (peaceful) *place in order to restore some order to his metabolism* (the chemical processes of the body). He wasn't sure why he felt physically ill and thought it may have been the result of the *steaming concoction* (mixture of things that don't go well together) of his emotions, his hormones, his thoughts and the coffee and cigarettes he had had, but he felt that he was forced to find a quiet place where he could start to feel better physically.

35 D He felt that he had been *duped* (tricked, deceived and therefore made to appear foolish) when he had seen mother and baby together because he had realized then that people *made such a big deal of fatherhood* (made it seem like something really important) simply because *it was such an implausible* (hard to believe) *state*, and he had realized that fathers were in fact *optional extras, accessories* (things which you can choose to have to accompany something but which do not have to be additions to them if you don't want them). In other words, he had previously thought that people 'made a big deal of fatherhood' because it was in fact important, but he now realized that

they made a big deal of it because it was totally unimportant and so they wanted to make it seem important.

36 A We are told that the books had warned him that he would feel that his role as a father was nothing more than a *footnote* (in this context, an unimportant detail) and that he would have a feeling of *irrelevance* (unimportance in relation to the subject) *and superfluity* (being additional and not required). The books had told him that he would get over this feeling but he had realized that this feeling was natural because it was indeed *manifestly* (very clearly), *poignantly* (in a way that causes a feeling of sadness) *true* that fathers were irrelevant and that he would only get over it if he stopped thinking about it. He therefore felt that it was not something that he would come to believe over a period of time was not true, it was something that would always be true and that the only way he could deal with it was by deliberately not giving any thought to it.

PART 6 2 MARKS PER QUESTION (TOTAL 14)

37 G At the beginning of G, the conversation between the two begins with the chairman asking the writer what he can do for him, in other words what the purpose of the writer's visit is. The writer then describes the chairman, saying that he had an indefinable polish (sophistication that it is hard to describe precisely) that only rich and famous people have. The paragraph after the gap begins with the writer's reply to the question asked by the chairman at the beginning of G.

38 E In the first sentence of E, *this* refers to what the writer has said about wanting more information about the club in the paragraph before the gap. The chairman, having considered it, says that there are several sources of information about the club and lists some. The writer then says that when he says this, the chairman sounds like a politician saying he believes in open government (a government that is honest with the people and gives them information rather than keeping it secret) but in fact giving nothing way (revealing no secrets, not providing information). In the first sentence after the gap, the writer says that he didn't want to be fobbed off (given an answer that is not adequate in order to get rid of him) and this links with his view at the end of E that the chairman was giving nothing away. In the paragraph after the gap, *They*, mentioned twice, refers back to the sources of information the chairman lists in E.

39 D At the beginning of D, the writer is interrupted by the chairman's mobile phone ringing. The beginning of the first sentence *As I was speaking* refers to his speech about sources of information about clubs in the paragraph before the gap. Immediately after the gap, *that* refers to the information about the club's attempt to buy a player that the chairman has revealed to the writer in D. He says that he has a little hope that the chairman will agree to this proposal because he has just been so open – this refers back to him giving what might have been considered private information about the attempt to buy a player in D.

40 H The writer clearly feels at this point that the chairman might consider his idea unacceptable. The first sentence of H means 'I had said what I came to say' and refers back to what he says he wants to be allowed to do for his book in the paragraph before the gap. In the first sentence after the gap *it* refers to the pitch mentioned at the end of H.

41 C At the beginning of C, the chairman reacts to the information given by the writer in the previous paragraph. At the start of the paragraph after the gap, the writer fears that he is starting to babble (talk incoherently, talk quickly and in a way that it hard to understand or follow) – this refers back to the many things he tells the chairman, one after the other without the chairman saying anything himself, in C.

42 F At the beginning of F, *Not at all* refers back to what he feared might happen in the paragraph before the gap, and the writer is saying that he certainly wasn't thrown out by the chairman. Immediately after the gap, the chairman says that a book about the club is a good idea. This refers back to and contrasts with what he says at the end of F – he is saying that although a TV series is not a good idea, a book is.

43 B In B, the chairman responds to what the writer says at the end of the paragraph before the gap – that he is being 'open-minded' – by saying that he is taking this attitude because the club has nothing to hide. In the final paragraph, the chairman responds to the writer's comment that supporters know how emotional football is by telling him that he means something more than that. In this phrase, *that* refers to the emotions that supporters have, as mentioned in B. The chairman is saying that the writer will find out that football is an amazingly emotional business in a way that is more complicated than simply the emotions of supporters.

PART 7 1 MARK PER QUESTION (TOTAL 10)

44 C When Morris got the information from his study of people who worked on buses, he *thought he might be on to something* (thought he might have discovered something important) *but it was still too early to say: he had to wait for other data to arrive*. So he was cautious about what he could conclude from the first set of information and wanted to see if it matched the other data.

45 B People move less because *labour-intensive jobs have disappeared* and they *live in an increasingly sedentary world* (life involves more and more sitting down). This is true both at work and in leisure time.

46 A Levine was not sure how he could measure people's movements during an average day and then he *hit upon a radical plan* (he suddenly thought of an unconventional way of doing it) – he gave specially sensored underwear to his volunteers. This underwear had sensors in it that measured all of their movements.

47 C When Morris got the information about bus workers, *To begin with, this didn't make sense*. At first, he could see no reason for the difference between drivers and conductors because they were the same age and ate the same food. Then he realized that the conductors moved a lot more than the drivers.

48 C People *slowly began to concede* that Morris really was onto something – he really had made an important discovery about the relationship between exercise and health. At first his peers responded to his paper with *hoots of derision* (they laughed at it and thought his conclusions were ridiculous) but gradually people began to accept that his conclusions were correct.

49 B The writer says that people in general *know that exercise is good for us and that sitting down all day isn't* but they *choose to ignore it* – they know they should do exercise but they don't actually do it.

50 D When Levine invented his device that would enable people to work and exercise at the same time, some people thought he had *completely flipped* (gone totally mad). But television stations did reports on it, and this caused people to think he was not nutty (mad). So the television stations did not think the idea was mad, although some other people did at first.

51 D When Levine put a tray on top of a treadmill, and set the treadmill to move at a slow speed, he was surprised to find that he *could work perfectly easily while he was walking along* and that he could *do almost everything that he normally did*

ANSWER KEY

CAMBRIDGE ENGLISH: PROFICIENCY PRACTICE TESTS ANSWER KEY 105

ANSWER KEY

sitting down. This meant that his idea of creating a device that would allow people to work and exercise at the same time was a practical and reasonable one.

52 **A** The writer says that Levine is *no stranger to weird experiments* – has previously carried out other strange experiments. An example of his unusual approach is the experiment involving snails that he did when he was 10 years old.

53 **B** The writer says that the idea that sitting down is *not just bad for people – it's a killer* could be regarded as *a bit drastic* (rather extreme). However, the writer says that this isn't the case, as many scientists believe that this view is correct.

Writing

MARK SCHEMES
MARKS OUT OF 20 FOR EACH QUESTION
ASSESSMENT CRITERIA ARE ON PAGE 92.

QUESTION 1

Content
The essay should include a summary of these four key points:
Text 1 (a) at first, the majority of people were not part of the youth culture
(b) later, youth culture and the cult of youth became dominant
Text 2 (a) youth culture involves exploiting the young for financial gain
(b) youth culture involves real innovation/is a real expression of what it is to be young

Communicative Achievement
This is an essay and so the register should be neutral or formal. The reader should be clear both as to what the key points in each text are and the candidate's own opinions and responses to those points.

Organization
The essay should be coherently organized in paragraphs, with clear linking between the summaries of the key points and the candidate's own views. An introduction and conclusion are not essential.

Language
The essay should contain an appropriate level of accurate grammar and vocabulary. Vocabulary connected with the topics of youth and fashion should be correctly used, as should grammatical structures for describing and comparing points of view/information, presenting and supporting opinions, and linking points in complex sentences.

QUESTION 2

Content
Report should include:
* list of social problems to be covered in the programme
* causes of those problems
* consequences of those problems

Communicative Achievement
Formal or neutral register, as appropriate for report by employee for employer. Report format, with clear sections and headings for them. Reader would understand fully and clearly what the writer believes should be included in the programme and how the items on the list should be presented.

Organization
Report should be structured so that each item listed is explained in terms of what the problem is, what causes it and the repercussions of it, with appropriate linking between these elements and perhaps between different items on the list.

Language
Language of description, analysis and suggestion.
FOR A SAMPLE ANSWER AND ASSESSMENT OF IT, SEE PAGE 127.

QUESTION 3

Content
Review should inform the reader about the event chosen, together with how it differed from the writer's expectations and what led to those expectations.

Communicative Achievement
Register should be appropriate for a review of this kind, and could be informal, formal or neutral but should be consistent throughout. Review should be appropriately paragraphed. Reader would have a clear picture of the event, the writer's expectations and views.

Organization
Clear development from description and narration of the event to comment on it, with appropriate linking between these elements.

Language
Language of narration, description and comparison, together with language appropriate for expressing views and feelings.

QUESTION 4

Content
Letter should describe one or more of the customs common in the candidate's country, together with why outsiders may consider it/them strange and views on it/them of others in the candidate's country.

Communicative Achievement
Register can be informal, formal or neutral, depending on the standpoint the candidate wishes to take to the topic. Standard letter format, but no addresses required. Reader

would have a clear understanding of what the custom or customs involve, and would be clear as to why it might be considered strange and what people actually think of it.

Organization

Brief introduction, explaining reason for writing letter and specifying custom or customs chosen. Brief conclusion for impact. Appropriate paragraphing, with clear linking between description of custom and both possible and real attitudes to it.

Language

Language of description and narration, and possibly comparison, together with language appropriate for expressing and supporting views.

Listening

PART 1 1 MARK PER QUESTION (TOTAL 6)

1 **C** The presenter says that if you *freak* (react strongly, in this case become very upset or angry) when your car won't start and if you are *tired of having to turn to your boyfriend* (are frustrated and annoyed by having to ask your boyfriend for help) *every time the engine splutters* (makes a noise suggesting it is not working properly), the course mentioned is *a must* (something that has to be done, something essential). She is clearly addressing women.

2 **B** She says that the mechanic was impressed when she told him about the course and that, as a result of taking it, *they* (mechanics) *can't rip me off now* (cheat her financially, deliberately overcharge her).

3 **B** The receptionist says that she replies with *heavy sarcasm* (saying emphatically the opposite of what she means in order to express annoyance or criticism) that she and her colleagues are *fairly useless* but *you never know* (you can't be absolutely sure), *it's a long shot* (something unlikely to happen but worth trying anyway), *but give it a whirl* (try it as an experiment, because it might succeed). In other words, she agrees with these people that she probably can't help them, but tells them that it's worth them asking if she can, although she is being sarcastic when she says this.

4 **A** She gives the example of someone phoning her and at the same time telling someone else a story, with the result that they can't remember who it is they have phoned. She says that in situations like that, it is polite to wait until *they've got a grip* (got the situation under control so that they know what they are doing) before continuing the conversation. However, she says that it is *far more satisfying to ring off* (end the call by putting the phone down) before that person has managed to remember why they have phoned. She clearly

means that this is not polite but that it is what she would like to do.

5 **B** The speaker says that it is *particularly English* (especially true of English people) to eat outdoors on *high days and holidays* (special occasions) *whatever the weather* (even if the weather is bad). Her question beginning *Who has not seen* means 'it is very common to see' and she says that it is typical to see English people in macs (raincoats) sitting *bizarrely* (doing something that is very strange and very hard to understand) *under dripping trees* (with rain falling in drops from them), *glumly* (with serious and unhappy expressions on their faces) sharing tea and crisps. She therefore says that English people looking unhappy while having picnics is a common sight.

6 **A** The speaker says that the sandwich, which is the essential basis of a picnic and was invented by and named after a member of the aristocracy, is an *evocative* (producing strong images, memories or feelings) and *much-maligned* (frequently spoken of with great dislike and disapproval) *food icon* (symbol, thing considered of great significance by many people). Her point therefore is that people see the sandwich as an important kind of food, and even though many people don't like it, it has powerful associations for many people.

PART 2 1 MARK PER QUESTION (TOTAL 9)

7 **sack of bricks**

In his first experiment, he tied a sack of bricks round his waist and he was also attached to a rope, but he does not say that the rope was round his waist.

8 **going to the moon**

He says that when he started diving, it was not common for people to go underwater and that going into a different environment (under water) was a challenge in the same way that going to the moon was.

9 **fire(-)fighting**

In the Army, the equipment he used for diving was modified (changed, adapted for a different purpose) fire-fighting equipment.

10 **sharks**

He says that he has *always felt uneasy* (nervous, anxious) *around* (when close to) *sharks*.

11 **marble slab**

He says that he made his worst mistake when he was diving near Cyprus and saw an ancient *marble* (a kind of hard stone used often for buildings and statues and often considered impressive) *slab* (large, thick, flat piece of stone), which he then tried to bring to the surface.

12 lungs; limbs

He says that he came to the surface too fast and that as a result he could hear *rattling* (short, sharp sounds, as of something hitting against something else repeatedly) in his lungs and his *limbs stopped working*.

13 crane

He says he had another bad moment while trying to *raise a crane* (a machine with a long arm that is used for lifting heavy objects, especially in construction work) that was stuck in mud in a harbour.

14 roof of a cave

He says that while he was testing a certain device in Florida, he touched the wrong controls and *shot* (went very quickly) into the roof of a cave.

15 conservation

He says that he is particularly interested in the conservation side (the aspects of diving that are concerned with taking care of natural things and creatures) and gives as an example of this his belief that killing fish results in the numbers of fish being depleted (reduced enormously so that there are not many or not enough left).

PART 3 1 MARK PER QUESTION (TOTAL 5)

16 A Diana clearly feels that her friend should have honoured the agreement that they made and that her refusal to give Diana the washing machine is not fair to Diana. Her friend has broken the agreement, by which Diana used her name in order to put two entries into the competition (one with her name on it, the other with her friend's name on it) and her friend agreed to give Diana the prize if the entry with her name on it won. Diana feels that this is wrong and unfair to her. She wonders too whether it may be legally wrong and whether consulting a lawyer would result in her getting what she regards as fair treatment.

17 D Kathy says that if she went to a lawyer, she wouldn't have *even the faintest chance* of forcing her friend to give her the prize and that legally she *doesn't have a leg to stand on* (she is completely in the wrong, there is nothing at all to support her case). She says that *the law would take a very dim view* (disapprove very strongly) of her situation because she has tried to *evade the rules* (break them by doing something that does not conform with the official requirements) of the competition and in doing so she has acted with *premeditated fraudulent intent* (these are legal terms meaning 'the crime of deliberate, planned in advance intention to cheat for financial or material gain'). In other words, she could get into trouble if she took legal action because she has herself done something illegal.

18 C Ron asks whether people who run competitions keep a *blacklist* (a list of people not allowed to do something, that is kept by an organization) containing the names of people who often win competitions and who the organization will not allow to win any more competitions. He wonders whether, if they do keep such lists, people like him should use *aliases* (false names) when entering competitions. Kathy says that it is natural for people who often win competitions but then go through a period of not winning any to get *paranoid* (wrongly believing that they are being intentionally badly treated) and suspect that such lists exist. However, she says that *no reputable* (respected, considered honourable) *firm would even contemplate* (consider) *such a measure* (action). The only exception to this is competitions run by shops, where there is *a faint* (very small) risk of the manager of a particular shop deciding to *deliberately disregard* (intentionally ignore) an entry from someone who he knows often wins competitions. But in *mainstream* (conventional, available to people in general) *competitions*, she says *such worries* (that blacklists are kept) *are groundless* (without foundation, not based on good reasons), and there is no reason for someone to use false names when entering them. In other words, she is saying that it is rare for the organizers of a competition to have a blacklist and therefore it is rare for the idea of using an alias to be logical.

19 C Stan knows his answer was correct but the answer sent to him by the organizers when he *sent for* it (wrote to them and asked for it) was completely different from his and therefore wrong. He has phoned to ask whether he has *grounds* (good reasons) *to make a formal objection* (complain formally).

20 B Kathy says that in this competition, the key (most important) word is 'estimate' because people have been asked to give an approximate figure not an accurate one. She says that it is therefore likely that the answer given by the people running the competition is also a guess, not an accurate figure. Their answer is therefore factually incorrect but it has to be accepted as the right answer because the rules of the competition state that 'the judges' decision is final' (it cannot be disputed). People entering the competition have agree to *abide by* (accept and obey) the rules and so they have to accept the answer given, even if it is wrong, as it is in this case. Her point therefore is that, although it might seem unfair that a wrong answer has to be accepted as right and therefore a correct answer does not win, this situation is covered by the rules and so no rules have been broken.

PART 4   1 MARK PER QUESTION (TOTAL 10)

21 G The speaker says that he *slogged away* (worked hard over a period of time) *without much of a break to get it all done* (to complete some work) before a meeting. He thought while he was doing this that there wasn't *any point doing it* (it was a waste of time and effort), and this proved correct because the matter was not discussed in the meeting.

22 H The speaker mentions someone who *thinks he can tell everyone else off* (criticize them for doing the wrong things) and says that she and her colleagues have discovered *to their cost* (it has caused them problems) that people *get in even more trouble* if they argue with this person. So the speaker is talking about a manager and this manager *made a big thing about how badly I'd done the work* (criticized her very strongly for it).

23 D The speaker says that he has been *singled out* (specially chosen) to represent the company at a trade fair. He did not expect this to happen (*I never thought they'd choose me*) and had *assumed there were far better candidates*. It is a good opportunity for him – it *will stand me in very good stead* (be very useful to me in the future) and *might lead to other things*.

24 B The speaker describes a discussion in which the other person gave her opinion on the speaker's *performance in recent times*. This discussion begins with the other person asking the speaker for her own opinion of how she had *been doing recently*. The other person both praised her and talked about ways in which she could improve.

25 E The speaker says that *everything went through smoothly* (everything was agreed without a problem) and *the whole thing was over in next to no time* (it only lasted for a short time). So the speaker is describing a meeting in which there was no disagreement.

26 H The speaker feels that the work he did *might very well prove to have been worth it eventually* – in the future it will be valuable. He thinks that it is likely that they will *go ahead with the project before too long* – the project he did the work for will happen. So he is hopeful that his work will be used in the future.

27 F The speaker says that when the person criticizes her, *I never let it get to me* (I do not allow the criticism to affect or upset me). She says that it *doesn't bother* her (it does not worry or upset her). She knows what this person is like and reacts to criticism from him in a relaxed way.

28 B The speaker says that the thought of going to the trade fair to represent the company *fills me with a certain amount of dread* (makes him rather nervous, gives him a feeling of fear). He is worried about it because he thinks he may not be *ready for it* and he is anxious that he might *mess it up* (do it very badly).

29 C The speaker says that she thought the discussion was a *very good piece of management* and so she was impressed by the way that person spoke, balancing praise with reference to how the speaker could improve.

30 D The speaker had expected that there would be *lots of arguments* because the people involved usually dislike each other and he *can't work out* (understand or explain) why the meeting *went so well* (was so successful). This *doesn't make sense* and the speaker can't see a *logical reason* for it.

TEST 3

Reading & Use of English

PART 1   1 MARK PER QUESTION (TOTAL 8)

1 C If someone **winces**, the muscles of their face twist sharply and briefly because they are experiencing pain, embarrassment or unhappiness.

A If someone **leers at** someone, they look at them with an expression on the face that makes it clear that they find them sexually attractive, and the other person or someone watching finds this unpleasant.

B If someone **squints**, they look at something with great effort and with the eyes partly shut, because the light in front of them is very bright or because their eyesight is poor.

D If someone **smirks**, they smile in a way that is considered unpleasant by someone who sees them do it, because it indicates that the person doing it finds something ridiculous or is in some way pleased with themselves.

2 B If a machine or appliance is **turned up full** or **on full**, its controls have been turned to the highest setting (volume, speed, temperature, etc.) so that it is operating at its greatest capacity.

A **Up top** is an informal expression meaning 'in the head' or 'on the head' and is used for talking about whether someone is intelligent or not or whether they have hair on their head or not.

C The **maximum** setting, speed, volume, temperature etc. of a machine or appliance is the highest level at which it can operate.

ANSWER KEY

D A **peak** is the point or time at which something is as high or intense as it can be or higher or more intense than it has ever been.

3 **A** If someone or something is **on the verge of something/doing something**, they are close to doing it or about to do it.

B The **rim** of something is the edge or border of something that is circular or round, such as a wheel or cup.

C The **fringe(s)** of something is the outer edge of an area, or a status close to inclusion in but not included in a group of people or the activities of a group of people ('people on the fringe(s) of the music business').

D A **border** is a strip on the edge of or around a photograph or piece of material that is intended to make it look pleasantly arranged. If something **borders on** something, it is close to being it ('a suggestion that borders on the ridiculous').

4 **C** If something **moves past** something, it moves from one side of it to the other and is then not next to or in front of it.

A If something **is beside** something, it is positioned next to it and not moving.

B If something **moves along** something, it moves on the surface of it and follows the shape of it.

D If something **moves across** something, it moves on the surface of it from one side to the other.

5 **A** The **prospect of something/doing something** is the idea of something that will or might happen in the future or the chance that something will happen.

B Someone's **outlook** on life, etc., is their general attitude towards it. The **outlook for** something is its probable future, what is likely to happen with regard to it.

C **Foresight** is the ability to predict what might happen so that you are ready to deal with it if it happens, or careful planning for the future based on considering what the circumstances might be then.

D A **viewpoint** is an opinion or attitude, or a point of view.

6 **D** If you **lay hands on** something, you get or obtain something that you have been looking for and want to find. The writer is saying that if she met Brennan, she would be like a historian who had found a source of information that no other historian had found.

A If you **set foot in** a place, you enter or arrive in the place.

B If you **rest** part of the body on something, you place it on that thing so that it is supported by it.

C If you **cast an/your eye over** something, you look at, inspect or read it briefly.

7 **B** If you **have a picture of** someone/something in your mind, you imagine what that person/thing looks like, although this may not be the way they really look. The writer is saying that Elizabeth did not have a clear idea of what Brennan would look like, although she had been given a general idea.

A The **sight of** something is the act or experience of seeing it.

C If you **have a vision/visions of** something, you imagine a situation, especially an unlikely or dramatic situation.

D Someone's **figure** is their physical shape or the outline of their body.

8 **C** The phrase **judging from** is used to introduce the reason or evidence on which a view or conclusion has been based. The writer is saying that Elizabeth thought that Brennan was going to be in a very weak and bad condition because of old age, because that was the impression the matron had given her.

A If you **reflect on** something, you think deeply about it for a period of time.

B If something **accounts for** something, it explains it or provides the reason for it. If you **take something into account**, you consider it before making a decision.

D How you **rate** something is the way you think of it in terms of the quality or value you think that it has.

PART 2 1 MARK PER QUESTION (TOTAL 8)

9 **between**
Between + a time + and + another time = during the period beginning with the first time and ending with the second time.

10 **Having**
The participle clause *Having lain derelict* is used here to say that one thing happened before another. 'Lain' is the past participle of 'lie' and if a place 'lies derelict', it remains unused and in a very poor state of disrepair for some time.

11 **fill**
If you *fill in* a form, etc., you write the information requested or required in the spaces provided on that form, etc.

12 **they**
This refers back to the *desperate people* mentioned earlier in the sentence. The writer is saying that the immigrants were people whose circumstances were terrible and that they had to fill in forms in English, even though they were not confident when using the language. In this context, 'whatever' means 'the unknown amount of' and 'halting' means 'hesitant, lacking in confidence'.

13 As/When/While/Whilst
The writer is talking about something that happens during the journey by boat to Ellis Island and during arrival there. The route described in this and the previous sentence is clearly the one taken by everyone going by ferry to Ellis Island and so 'If' would not fit here.

14 not
The writer is saying that when you approach and arrive at Ellis Island, nobody can avoid thinking deeply about the experience of the immigrants in the same place in the past.

15 how
The phrase *how it must have looked* could also be 'what it must have looked like'. The writer is talking about the impression of the place that the immigrants got from its appearance when they arrived there.

16 to
If someone *clings to/onto someone/something*, they hold on tightly to it/them.

PART 3 1 MARK PER QUESTION (TOTAL 8)

17 deceptive
If something is **deceptive**, it is not what it appears to be or it creates a false impression.

18 contender
If someone is a **contender for** something such as a prize, an award or a title, they are in competition for it with others but they might win it.

19 allegedly
This means 'claimed by others to be the case but not actually proved to be the case'. The adverb form is required because the word qualifies the verb phrase 'behaving badly'.

20 traumatized/traumatised
This is the past participle of the verb traumatize and is in the passive form. It means 'caused to be in a state of enormous shock and unhappiness'.

21 unconventional
If something is **unconventional**, it is unusual and not considered normal or typical by people in general.

22 assignments
An **assignment** is a task that someone has to carry out as part of their job, when they have the sort of job that involves completing a particular task and then going on to another, separate task. In this context, the 'assignments' are particular authors that particular publicists have to deal with.

23 colourful
If something is **colourful**, it is interesting and striking rather than dull or predictable. In this context, we can infer that the writer means that the feminist writer's language when shouting at her publicists includes swear words and insults.

24 survivor
If someone is a **survivor of** something, they have had an unpleasant experience, but they have continued to exist as they did before that, rather than being destroyed by the experience. The writer is talking about someone who worked with the thriller writer on a tour together and who, despite this terrible experience, is still a publicist.

PART 4 2 MARKS PER QUESTION (TOTAL 12)

25 creative (1 mark)
takes her mind off (1 mark)
To follow 'being', the verb 'creating' has to be changed to the adjective 'creative'.
If something *takes your mind off something*, it stops you from thinking about something unpleasant or worrying because it causes you to direct your thoughts and attention to it instead.

26 getting/becoming (1 mark)
mixed up in (1 mark)
The verb 'avoid' is followed by the '-ing' form of another verb.
If you *get/become mixed up in something*, you become involved in something that you don't wish to get involved in or that it is a bad idea to get involved in.

27 on to deny (1 mark)
(that) he had done/doing/having done anything (1 mark)
If someone *goes on to do something*, they do a second thing after completing a first thing.
If you *deny* something, you say that it is not true or not the case. The verb is used with the following structures: *deny + (that) ... ; deny + -ing; deny + having + past participle; deny + noun.*

28 to seek advice OR to go and seek advice (1 mark)
from an (1 mark)
If you are *forced to do* something, you have to do it, either because of circumstances or because someone else has given you the obligation to do it.
The structure *seek + uncountable noun* means 'ask for something' or 'try to get something'. The verb *advise* has to be changed to the noun advice.
If the person or place that might provide the thing that someone seeks is mentioned, this is preceded by the preposition from.

29 no fault of my own (1 mark)
I found (1 mark)
The phrase *through no fault of someone's own* is used for saying that something bad happened to someone but that they were not responsible for the fact that it happened.
If you *find yourself* in a particular situation, you become aware of the fact that you are in that situation, especially when you feel that it is a situation that you did not create yourself.

30 for computing (1 mark)
in preference to (1 mark)
If you *opt for something*, you choose it, especially as a result of careful thought.
The linking phrase *in preference to* means 'rather than' when saying that the subject prefers one thing to another.

PART 5 2 MARKS PER QUESTION (TOTAL 12)

31 C The writer says that the audience for the programme was a *broad* (containing a wide range of people) one and that *none of the usual rigid divisions and omissions* (the fact that some kinds of people didn't watch certain programmes and were therefore 'missing' from the audience) were apparent in it. He says that audiences for programmes usually had *stark* (very clear) *class bias* (the majority of an audience belonged to a particuar social class), *gender imbalance* (far more men than women in the audience or far more women than men), *obvious age asymmetry* (not an equal number of people from all age groups but more people belonging to one age group than another) or *generalized demographic slant* (general tendency for an audience to consist of more people fitting into certain categories than people fitting into other categories). This audience had none of these factors. His point is that different types of programme usually appealed to different types of person but that this programme was watched by all types. The implication is that some types of people would not have been expected to watch a programme of this kind but in fact they did, because all types of person watched it.

32 A The writer says that they were a *double-act* (a pair of entertainers who perform together), that each of them was *half a star* and that as a couple they were *a whole star*. He does not say that they were both stars individually or that as a couple they were two stars, and so the implication is that they were highly successful as a couple but that they would not have been stars if they had been individual performers.

33 D The writer says that the programme *came to stand for* (be a symbol of, represent) *excellence in broadcasting* not only because of *two gifted performers* but also because of a *richly proficient* (highly skilled) *and supremely committed* (caring enormously) *production team* (group of people responsible for making a programme). These people therefore made a very significant contribution in his view to the programme becoming one that *stood for something greater,*

something far more precious than mere (simply) *first-rate* (excellent) *but evanescent* (soon disappearing from the memory) *entertainment* and they were an important factor in it having been popular *for the previous nine years or so.*

34 B The writer says that he fears that the programme is *fast assuming the aura of a fairy tale* (quickly beginning to have the quality of a story told to children about people and things that never really existed) and that it is *destined to be* (it cannot be prevented from being) *passed on with bemused* (confused) *fascination from one doubtful generation to its even more disbelieving successor.* His point is that in future people (in this case, he probably means programme-makers) will think that it wasn't really as popular or as good as they are told it was.

35 C The writer says that *no celebrated* (famous and respected) *guest was ever allowed to challenge this comic democracy* (treatment of people as equals), according to which Morecambe & Wise never *looked down on* (considered themselves superior to), *or up at* (considered themselves inferior to), *anyone*. These guests were therefore never treated with special respect and in the show, they *went unrecognized and frequently unpaid* – this was *a running gag* (a joke that continued and was repeated throughout the show). Guests who were *venerable* (old and highly respected) actors were *mocked* (made fun of, made to look foolish) *routinely* by Eric's sotto voce (in a low voice, quiet or whispered) *comments*. The writer is therefore saying that all guests appearing on the show, however famous they were, were made fun of on the show.

36 A The writer says that *instead of settling – as so many of their supposed successors would do with unseeemly haste – for the easy security of a 'cult following'* (instead of accepting that the best they could hope for was to be popular with a small group of enthusiasts, which is what comedians who came after and were considered to have filled the places of Morecambe and Wise did, quickly and wrongly), Morecambe and Wise always wanted to entertain the whole nation. He is therefore saying that comedians who it has been claimed have been their successors have preferred to gain a cult following quickly, because that is easier to do than to do what Morecambe and Wise did and try to appeal to the whole country.

PART 6 2 MARK PER QUESTION (TOTAL 14)

37 E In E, the account of what Rebus had done at the zoo before this point continues from the opening paragraph, and we learn about how he had reacted to seeing various creatures and how he was feeling. In the paragraph after the gap, we learn that before this occasion he hadn't been to the zoo for a long time, since he had taken his daughter there.

38 H In H, his visit with his daughter in the previous paragraph is contrasted with this occasion and *though* in the first sentence means 'unlike on that occasion', referring back to the visit with his daughter in the paragraph before the gap. Immediately after the gap, Not very refers back to the word conspicuous in H, and the first sentence after the gap means that he hoped that he wasn't very conspicuous. **39 D** At the start of D *Two more* refers back to the meerkats mentioned in the paragraph before the gap and means 'two more meerkats'. In the sentence immediately after the gap, *There were worse* refers back to the assignment mentioned in D and means that Rebus reminded himself that there were worse assignments in his job than zoo patrol (walking round the zoo looking out for someone or something).

40 F In F, we learn more about the case he is working on at the zoo, mentioned in the previous paragraph, including efforts that were being made to catch the person responsible and the fact that people wanted that person to be caught. In the paragraph after the gap, *Meantime* refers to the period during which the crimes have been going on and people have wanted the person responsible to be caught, as described in F.

41 A In the first sentence of A, *it* refers back to the meerkat den, mentioned in the last sentence of the paragraph before the gap and we learn that Rebus moves a short distance away from it. The paragraph after the gap continues on the subject of Rebus' attitude towards animals, which is mentioned at the end of A.

42 G In G, his attitude towards horses, cats and dogs, mentioned in the previous paragraph, is contrasted with his attitude towards the meerkats in the zoo. *On the other hand* links the two attitudes, and has the meaning 'Although he wasn't interested in horses, cats or dogs ...' In the sentence after the gap, we are told that if the role reversal described in G happened, it would not be an exact one. The word *Except* here has the meaning 'But the difference would be that ...' and we are told that the humans would behave like animals in a zoo do but that the animals wouldn't behave like the humans at a zoo do, because they *wouldn't share a human's*

curiosity (interest in finding out about things).

43 B In the first sentence of B, its subjects refers back to the camera mentioned in the paragraph before the gap and means 'the things the camera was being pointed at, the things that the camera was taking photos of'. In the final paragraph, we learn that Rebus knew who this man was but couldn't remember his name.

PART 7 1 MARK PER QUESTION (TOTAL 10)

44 C When she set up on her own, her idea of creating a brand of luxury jewellery that had an ethical basis *coincided with a gap in the market* – she did it at a time when there was a demand for such jewellery but nobody else was making and selling it.

45 C She says that she is *passionate that people understand the symbolism behind my work*. She doesn't want people to see her jewellery simply as objects, she wants them to know the story behind each piece.

46 A She says that if someone asks her *about an animal I haven't done*, she will then *introduce it to the collection* – she makes a piece of jewellery featuring that animal.

47 A When she told the girl who was wearing one of the rings she had made that she was the person who had made the ring, the girl became *star-struck* (strongly affected by meeting someone famous). The girl reacted to her as if she was a very important, famous person.

48 B She sometimes does not sell pieces that she makes because she becomes *emotionally involved* with them and so she wants to keep them and can't let go of them (part with them, let someone else have them). She puts thse pieces in what she calls 'the family museum'.

49 D She says that she is not creating jewellery that is *for the moment* (only of temporary interest, only to please someone in the present moment). She thinks that her pieces are classics in their own right, not trend-specific – they can be regarded as classic pieces because of their individual qualities, not as pieces that are part of a general fashion that will not last for a long time.

50 C Many of her pieces have a label on them that describe them as 'ecological' because they are made from gold that was extracted without the use of cyanide, which is bad for the environment. The label shows that her company is one of only a few that are certified (officially recognized) users of this kind of gold.

51 D She says that her style is *very individual and not for the faint-hearted* – she has an unusual style and some people may find it too extreme or unconventional, so that it requires some courage and confidence to wear it. She is suggesting that some people may not like it because of this.

52 **A** She usually makes jewellery showing animals but she also makes *engagement rings, not all animal-related. Bespoke commissions* (making individual things to meet a specific requirement) are *becoming more frequent* for her and some of these involve pieces that do not have animals and are therefore not like what she usually makes.

53 **C** She has *no plans for e-commerce*, because she believes this *detracts from* (reduces the value or importance of) *the meaning behind the piece*. She has decided that she will not start selling her jewellery on the internet.

Writing

MARK SCHEMES
MARKS OUT OF 20 FOR EACH QUESTION
ASSESSMENT CRITERIA ARE ON PAGE 92.

QUESTION 1

Content

The essay should include a summary of these four key points:

Text 1 (a) adults compare children's games today unfavourably with the games they played
(b) adults prevent children from creating their own games by giving them money

Text 2 (a) the way some children's games are played changes or varies
(b) some children's games disappear and new ones appear

Communicative Achievement

This is an essay and so the register should be neutral or formal. The reader should be clear both as to what the key points in each text are and the candidate's own opinions and responses to those points.

Organization

The essay should be coherently organized in paragraphs, with clear linking between the summaries of the key points and the candidate's own views. An introduction and conclusion are not essential.

Language

The essay should contain an appropriate level of accurate grammar and vocabulary. Vocabulary connected with the topics of games and childhood should be correctly used, as should grammatical structures for describing and comparing points of view/information, presenting and supporting opinions, and linking points in complex sentences.

QUESTION 2

Content

Letter should describe the unfair situation and how candidate became aware of it, explain the bad consequences of it and recommend appropriate action by the authorities.

Communicative Achievement

Register appropriate for a reader writing in to a newspaper about a serious matter – fairly formal or neutral. Standard letter format. Reader would understand writer's reasons for writing, views and recommendations fully and clearly.

Organization

Clear introduction, explaining reason for writing letter. Clear organization of points with appropriate paragraphing and conclusion.

Language

Language of narration (to give the background) and of description, analysis and recommendation (for expressing and supporting opinions).

QUESTION 3

Content

Report should include:
• causes of dissatisfaction in the department
• examples of incidents causing dissatisfaction
• recommendations for improving the situation that have come from the staff

Communicative Achievement

Register appropriate for an employee writing a report for someone in authority – formal or neutral. Report format, with clearly divided sections under clear subject headings. Reader would understand fully and clearly the causes of the dissatisfaction and the actions that the staff want to be taken.

Organization

The report should be well-structured with clear sections. Ideas should be presented in readable prose, although note-form may be appropriate in some parts. There should be appropriate linking between main points and exemplification of them and between main points and recommendations concerning them.

Language

Language of describing (the causes), narration (the incidents), analysing, recommending and hypothesizing.

QUESTION 4

Content

Article should describe the writer's ambition, explain what is/was involved in achieving it and describe the writer's attitude to risk.

Communicative Achievement

Candidate may opt for formal, informal or neutral register, but register should be consistent throughout.

Format suitable for an article – paragraphs may be brief for impact and may have sub-headings. Reader would understand precisely the nature of the ambition, what is involved in it and the writer's standpoint with regard to taking risks in life.

Organization
Clear development from description of ambition to narration of how to achieve it, to 'philosophizing' about attitudes to life, with appropriate linking between these elements and appropriate paragraphing.

Language
Language of description and narration, together with language appropriate for describing feelings and expressing opinions, as well as perhaps hypothesizing and suggesting.
FOR A SAMPLE ANSWER AND ASSESSMENT OF IT, SEE PAGE 128.

Listening

PART 1   1 MARK PER QUESTION (TOTAL 6)

1   B   She says that they were encouraged to live at *'grass-root' level* (have the same living conditions as ordinary people in the place, rather than a better standard because they were only there temporarily), and that in fact it was *impossible not to* (not to live this way) *on the meagre* (small and inadequate) *amount of pocket money* (money to spend for pleasure rather than on food, accommodation, etc.) *we were allotted* (given as a share of what is available). She is therefore saying that they were given so little money by the organization that had employed them that they had to live like the local people.

2   A   She says that living there meant *embracing the culture* (accepting and living according to it) *with open arms* (enthusiastically), and she then adds *whether you liked it or not*, which implies that she did not like having to embrace the culture. She says that the meat, soup and home-made beer *was not to be sampled but lived off*, which implies that she would have preferred to be able to eat and drink those things simply to find out what they were like rather than having to eat and drink them all the time. Furthermore, she says that she *could forget any vegetarian tendencies* (her desires to be vegetarian) because everyone there eats meat, which implies that she would have preferred not to have to eat meat but to have been vegetarian, but that she had to eat meat.

3   B   He says that in order to get an audience when performing on adventure playgrounds, they perform some distance away from the play equipment (so that the children will watch the performance rather than play on the equipment). He then says that in schools they *have to work harder to get a response* from the children. He is therefore saying that it is easier to get a response from children on adventure playgrounds than in schools. Children in schools *can be controlled*, unlike children on adventure playgrounds, who can leave if they don't like the performance, but he says that children in schools are harder to get a response from than children on adventure playgrounds.

4   C   He says that they *unmask* (reveal what they really look like by taking off make-up, costumes, etc.) as part of the process of *bringing the kids down* (making them less excited). He says this is very important because you should only involve children in *uninhibited* (not restricted, natural) *action if you can bring about* (cause to happen) *a return to 'normality' at the end*. Therefore, they appear as they normally do again so that children can return to what is normal for them at the end of the performance.

5   B   The speaker says boys are *unencumbered* (not burdened, free because of not carrying responsibility) *by all the baggage* (things that accompany and are difficult to deal with) *of adult lives* and can therefore *truly understand the nature of friendship*. His point is that boys can have real friendships because they do not have the kinds of things in their lives that prevent adults from having them.

6   C   He says that, although he can understand why his friendships as an adult have to have a certain amount of *formality* (follow certain procedures by which he arranges in advance to meet friends), he sometimes thinks that this is a *negation of* (the opposite of) friendship. He is therefore saying that the friendships he has now are not in his view what he believes real friendships to be.

PART 2   1 MARK PER QUESTION (TOTAL 9)

7   multi(-)use environment
The presenter says that the home, rather than being a place of *privacy, escape and retreat* (which all mean 'a place where you can be away from others'), is becoming a place that can have many uses or functions. He says that people who *come up with new jargon* (people who invent new technical or specialist words used in particular professions) might use this term to describe the home.

8   prints
In this context, *prints* are pictures or designs printed on a surface.

9 rent reduction

His flatmate was *less keen* than Johnny on members of the public walking around the flat on Sunday mornings and felt that, because this caused him inconvenience, the amount of rent he paid should be reduced.

10 Made to Measure

The name is a phrase used in the clothing industry to describe clothes that are individually made for someone after that person has been measured so that the clothes are of the correct size.

11 art consultant

This job presumably involves advising wealthy people and companies on what paintings, etc. to buy.

12 Private/private

Because visitors are fascinated by the house, they have put up signs indicating that certain parts of it cannot be visited – they want them to visit the gallery but they want them to keep out of the parts of the house where they live.

13 (genuine/real) velvet

Velvet is a fairly expensive fabric used for clothes and furnishings. Jasmine is emphasizing here that the fabric used is not something artificial that is supposed to look like velvet, it really is velvet.

14 coal cellar

A *cellar* is a room or area underground where certain things are stored. In this case, coal used to be kept there, in the days when coal was used for heating houses. Now, the equipment for showing films on a screen is kept there.

15 The Picturedome/The Picture Dome

A *dome* is a round roof with a circular base and in the past many cinemas had these. In this context, picture means 'film' or 'movie'.

PART 3 1 MARK PER QUESTION (TOTAL 5)

16 B   Martin says that a referee *worries most about his future* when he *stops getting letters and is no longer being booed outside football grounds*. The letters are those he has previously referred to, which contain *praise* and *sour* (hostile, angry) *abuse* (insults, rude and nasty remarks). If a group of people or a crowd 'boos', they show their disapproval or dislike of someone by shouting 'boo' loudly and repeatedly. He is therefore saying that referees worry if they stop getting these reactions.

17 D   Martin says that referees like to think that players respect them both for their *astuteness* (quality of being clever and perceptive) and their fairness. He says they are like schoolteachers who see themselves as being *close to the boys* (friendly with them rather than a distant, strict authority figure) or police detectives who think that *give-*

and-take (willingness to make compromises by which both sides tolerate each other) is the best way to deal with criminals. What he is saying is that they think that players respect them if they are not too strict with them but allow them to do some bad things without punishing them.

18 A   Martin's general point here is that it is wrong to see referees as people who have unselfish motives, because it is not *public-spiritedness* (the desire to provide the public with a service) that makes people want to be referees and *there is much more satisfying of ego than disinterest in the motive* (a major reason why people become referees is that they want to feel important). However, he does say that *there is undoubtedly a deep absorption in football here* (referees are certainly extremely enthusiastic about football). In other words, he is saying that they do have selfish motives, but that it would be wrong to think they aren't really extremely keen on football.

19 B   Martin says that *under these circumstances* (because of the system of assessment of referees), it is not *overstating* (exaggerating) *the referee's predicament* (difficult situation) to say that a referee has to have *a skin like a rhinoceros* (a rhinoceros has a thick skin and 'to be thick-skinned' means 'not to be sensitive to criticism') *and to be as deaf as a post* (this is an idiom meaning 'completely deaf' – in this context, it means 'to ignore criticism, not to listen to criticism'). His point is that they have to be like this because they are criticized by the crowd during the game and then they are criticized by their assessors after it.

20 C   Martin says that a referee should be able to *differentiate* (know the difference) *quickly between the spontaneous* (said without previous thought or planning) *expletives* (rude words, swear words) *of angered players and the malevolent* (said deliberately in order to upset) *abuse* (nasty remarks) *of those trying to intimidate him* (frighten him in order to influence what he does). He also says that there are times during games when *gamesmanship* (trying to win games by upsetting the opponent or by doing things which are not strictly according to the rules but do not actually break them) *and outright* (clear, open, without doubt) *villainy* (wicked, very bad behaviour) *test a referee to his limit* (put the maximum amount of pressure on a referee), and that a referee *has to decide instantly which of the two* (gamesmanship or outright villainy) *is present in an incident* (when something violent or controversial happens during a game that a referee must make a decision about). His point is that referees must decide 'quickly' whether players intend to intimidate them or are simply reacting automatically when they say nasty things to them, and they must decide 'instantly' whether players have truly bad intentions or are simply using 'gamesmanship' when there is an unpleasant incident during a game.

PART 4 1 MARK PER QUESTION (TOTAL 10)

21 H The speaker talks about a story that concerns something that is *potentially harmful* for people. This is an example of stories that tell people what they should do and shouldn't do. Some of these stories concern *bad consequences* for people. The speaker is clearly talking about stories concerning what is good and bad for people's health.

22 E The speaker talks about someone who appears to have *a good chance of taking over the leadership*. She is clearly talking about a politician becoming the leader of a political party because she says that this person wants to *do good for the majority* and this is the sort of person who people want to be *in charge* (in positions of power).

23 G The speaker talks about someone who is an example of people who *get all the wealth and all the attention*. This is a person who has *managed to rise to the top* (become successful) *with the aid of publicists* (people who are employed to put stories about them in the media).

24 C The speaker talks about something *horrible* that has happened and says that she feels sorry for the *victims*. She is clearly talking about a bad crime that has made people feel *worked up* (anxious, nervous) because of their fear that such a thing *could happen to them*.

25 A The speaker talks about a story that concerns *how people live these days*. It is about something that is happening among people *in general*, a *new trend* (a change in behaviour, habits or attitudes). It concerns a certain *lifestyle* and problems associated with it.

26 A The speaker says that he finds it hard to *take it seriously* (to accept and believe what is said in the news story) and that he is *inclined to doubt* (reacts by doubting) that the story is true. So the speaker is doubtful about the story, and says that such stories *contradict each other*, making them hard to believe in his opinion.

27 E The speaker says that this story *could represent something very good for the future* and says that it concerns someone who is *saying all the right things* in the speaker's opinion. The speaker is very

glad about this and can see no *downside* (negative aspect) to it.

28 D The speaker says that it *irritates* him (makes him angry) when people like this give their opinions on *what's going on in the country and the world*. He says that this person *talks adolescent rubbish* and it *infuriates* the speaker (makes him very angry) that people treat this person as if his opinions on such issues are important.

29 F The speaker says that she believes that *such incidents are very rare* and so she doesn't *let this kind of thing get to me* (she doesn't worry or get upset about it). She says that when these kinds of things happen, people *just have to carry on regardless* (ignore what has happened and continue with their lives in the normal way).

30 C The speaker says that he pays no attention to this story because it is about a lifestyle that most people don't have, one that is limited to a *privileged minority* that he doesn't belong to.

TEST 4

Reading & Use of English

PART 1 1 MARK PER QUESTION (TOTAL 8)

1 (D) If something **does the trick**, it succeeds in solving the problem it is intended to solve or in achieving the intended result.

   A If someone **pulls something off**, they succeed in doing something difficult when they were considered unlikely to be able to do it.

   B If someone or something **works a miracle/miracles**, they succeed in making something that did not appear likely to be successful into something very good or very successful.

   C If you **play a trick on** someone, you deceive them in order to make them look foolish or so that they will be laughed at.

2 (D) **Spending power** is the amount of money people or organizations have which is available to them to spend on things. The writer is saying that the big film companies have a lot of money to spend on publicising their films but that smaller companies don't.

   A **Market/economic forces** are things which have a big influence on a commercial market or on the economy of a country.

   B The **strength** of an economy or currency is how well it is doing in comparison with its situation in the past or the economies of other countries or other currencies.

C If someone or something **has/carries weight**, they are powerful in a certain context and have a great deal of influence.

3 (C) If someone **responds to** something, they react to it by doing something or they react in the way that they are intended to. Andrea Klein is talking about people who do not react to big advertising campaigns for films – they are not influenced by these campaigns and do not go to see films because of them.

A If someone **rises to** something, for example a challenge, they react to a difficult or demanding situation by doing what is required.

B If something **triggers** a reaction, it causes a sudden or strong reaction to happen.

D If something **stirs up** a feeling, it causes someone to have a strong feeling.

4 (A) If something is **killed stone dead**, it is completely destroyed.

B If someone is **flat broke**, they have absolutely no money at all.

C If you say something **point blank**, you say it directly without any attempt to be diplomatic, in a way that may be considered rude.

D If someone is **out cold**, they are unconscious, often as a result of being hit. If something, for example food or drink, is **stone cold**, it is completely cold when it should be warm.

5 (C) If someone is **not averse to** something, they are not opposed to it or they don't dislike it.

A If someone is **reluctant to do** something, they do not want to do it, although perhaps in the end they have to do it.

B If something is **counter to** something, it is in opposition to it.

D If someone is **obstinate**, they refuse to change their mind about something, despite attempts to persuade them to do so and despite the fact that they are wrong.

6 (A) If you **leave someone to do** something, you allow them to do it themselves, rather than doing it for them.

B If you **avail yourself** of something, for example an opportunity/offer, you take advantage of something that is available to you.

C If you **consent to something**, you formally or officially agree to it.

D If you **give someone the chance/opportunity/ freedom, etc. to do something**, you allow them to have it.

7 (B) If someone is **caught up in a vicious circle**, they are in a situation in which one problem results in another which makes the original problem even worse.

A If something is **relentless**, it is unpleasant and it never stops, it is constant.

C If someone or something is **brutal**, they are very cruel and show no pity.

D If someone or something is **merciless**, they cause suffering and show no pity when doing so.

8 (C) If someone **recovers their costs**, they get back the money they have spent in order to do something, although they may not actually make a profit.

A If someone **restores something to someone**, they give it back to them after it has been lost or taken from them.

B If someone **refunds someone/ something**, they return to them money they have spent, for example because they did not receive exactly what they had paid for.

D If someone **reimburses someone for something**, they give them back money they have spent.

PART 2 1 MARK PER QUESTION (TOTAL 8)

9 **Such**
In this context, *Such* means 'So great'. It is used at the beginning of the sentence with the verb and subject inverted (the verb is before the subject) for emphasis.

10 **ourselves**
The reflexive is used here because the writer is saying that people in the future will watch their own lives on television all the time, rather than watching other people.

11 **the**
The definite article is used here because the writer is using singular nouns to represent all examples of something. What is meant here is that 'the audience for each programme of the kind just described is the star of each of those programmes' – the people watching such programmes are the same as the people appearing in them.

12 **can**
The writer's point here is that, in the 'inclusive culture' described, it is possible for any person to make, take part in and perform in a TV programme.

13 **what**
The question *What is the point of something/doing something?* means 'What is the value or purpose of it?' In this case, the question is rhetorical, because the writer is making a point rather than asking a genuine question.

14 **there**
The writer's point here is that if everyone can take part in culture, that culture loses its quality of being interesting and attractive. *There* has to be used as the subject of the verb.

15 To

The infinitive is used here as the subject of the first clause of the sentence. The writer is saying that it would be wrong for him to believe it was automatically true that he could try to do what someone he regards as a genius and loves listening to can do.

16 would

This part of the sentence is like the second part of a conditional structure. The sentence could be 'If I assumed then that I could 'have a go' at their craft, this/it would be monstrous impudence on my part'.

PART 3 1 MARK PER QUESTION (TOTAL 8)

17 descendants

Someone's *descendants* are the generations of their species or family that come after them.

18 ease

If you do something with ease, you do it easily, without a lot of effort because you know how to do it and you are good at doing it.

19 necessity

If something is a *necessity*, it is essential.

20 upgrading

If you *upgrade* equipment, you add something to it or replace it, so that what you have is up to date with regard to the latest developments in equipment of that kind.

21 visually

This means 'to look at', 'when looked at' or 'in appearance'.

22 signify

In this context, this means 'indicate', 'show' or 'mean'..

23 persuasive

If something that someone says is *persuasive*, it makes people hearing it believe that it is or may be true.

24 advantageous

This means 'favourable' or 'beneficial'. If something is 'seen, put, etc. in a certain light', it appears that way.

PART 4 2 MARK PER QUESTION (TOTAL 12)

25 myself (that) (1 mark)
there was nothing to fear/there wasn't/was not anything to fear/I had nothing to fear (1 mark)

If you *satisfy yourself (that) something is the case*, you make sure or confirm that you are right to believe that it is the case. In this sentence, *fear* has to be a verb (rather than a noun), and the structure 'there was no reason to be + adjective' has to be transformed into the structure *there was nothing/wasn't anything + infinitive or I had nothing + infinitive*.

26 was singled out (1 mark)
for (1 mark)

If someone *singles someone/something out*, they mention or treat them as being different in some

way from all the others. The past simple active verb has to be transformed into the past simple passive here. The phrasal verb 'single out' is followed by *for + noun* to say in what way the person is spoken of or treated differently from others. In this sentence 'praise' is a noun.

27 unconvincing denial (of the accusation) (1 mark)
led me to (1 mark)

The possessive *His* in this sentence must be followed by an adjective and a noun, and so the adverb 'unconvincingly' must be changed to the adjective 'unconvincing' and the verb 'denied' must be changed to the noun 'denial'. If 'denial' is followed by a noun, the preposition 'of' must come after 'denial' and before the noun. If something *makes you think that something is true*, it leads you to believe it. The relative clause in the first sentence must be replaced by a verb clause, since the first part of the sentence is now a subject ('His unconvincing denial') rather than a complete clause.

28 reached/got to a/the stage when/where (1 mark)
I had no (1 mark)

The phrase *subject + reach/get to + the/a + stage + when/where* means that, after a period of time when something has continued, there is a point in time when something happens that changes the situation. The structure *run out of + noun* has to be transformed into the structure *have + no more + noun + left*.

29 is liable to (1 mark)
have a (1 mark)

The structure *subject + be liable + infinitive* = 'it + be likely + that + subject + verb' or 'subject + be likely + infinitive'. If someone *has a fit*, they become extremely angry or shocked and show that they feel this way by shouting, etc.

30 lack of experience/inexperience (1 mark)
counted against her (1 mark)

In this sentence, the possessive *Her* must be followed by a noun, and so the adjective *inexperienced* must be changed to the noun *inexperience* or to the noun phrase *lack of experience*. If something *counts against someone*, it is considered a negative aspect concerning them when a decision or judgement is being made about them.

PART 5 2 MARKS PER QUESTION (TOTAL 12)

31 B The narrator says that the expression on his face seemed *amiable* (friendly) but she also says that she *squinted* (looked with the eyes narrowed, as if having difficulty seeing something) when she looked at him, probably because he had shouted to her from some distance away – he *hailed* (called or shouted to in order to attract her attention) her *from across the vast concrete* *expanse of the courthouse steps*. She therefore had some difficulty in seeing the expression on his face and so wasn't completely sure that he really did look friendly.

32 A She says that *to have Fat Mikey as a client was to have an annuity* (a regular annual income) and she gave him her card so that she might be able to have him as a client. The reason why any criminal defence lawyer (we learn in the second paragraph that she now was one, whereas before she had been a prosecutor) would like to have him as a client was that he was one of the three people involved in organized crime who the police *routinely picked up* (collected) for questioning on matters of Mob-related mayhem (violent behaviour connected with organized crime, groups of criminals such as the Mafia). A defence lawyer could therefore earn a lot of money from defending him, since he was so regularly accused of crimes, and she gave him her card because she was not unaware of that fact. (Note that this text comes from a US publication and so the US spelling of 'defense' is used.)

33 C The narrator says that at the trial she described Fat Mikey as *'a vulture* (a bird that waits for creatures to die and then eats them) *feasting* (eating energetically and with great pleasure) *on society's entrails* (internal organs)' in her *summation* (summary at the end of a court case), and for that reason it might have seemed *presumptuous* (too familiar, inappropriate because suggesting a closer relationship than the one that really existed) to call him 'Mike', as this might have been something his friends called him. Since she had described him in that way at the trial, she did not feel that she could now call him a name that suggested they were friends.

34 D Fat Mikey asked the narrator whether she thought she really could earn a living from defending people like him and asked her whether that kind of legal work had been what she *had had in mind* (been thinking of or intending) when she was training to be a lawyer. She said that it hadn't been and that she had been *leaning toward Eskimo fishing rights* (thinking that she would probably get involved in the kind of law that dealt with the legal rights of various groups of people) at that time. However she said that defending people like him was what she was good at. He showed that he disagreed by shaking his head at her *folly* (foolishness), and told her that *when a guy's ass is in a sling* (this is a slang term meaning 'when someone is in serious trouble'), he is unlikely to hire (employ as his lawyer) *a girl who says 'whom'*

(presumably because this is so grammatically correct that it would suggest to such a man that this lawyer would not be suitable for a case such as his, involving the sort of crimes not usually committed by educated people). She replies that *if he's partial to* (if he likes) *his ass he will*, meaning that if he wants to get out of trouble, he will engage a lawyer who speaks like that – the implication being that such people would employ her, since we already know that she spoke like that at Fat Mikey's trial.

35 C The narrator says that she was not the kind of attorney (lawyer in the US) who got *naughty thrills* (excitement caused by doing things they shouldn't do, behaving badly) *socializing with* (spending time outside work with) *hoods* (violent criminals), although it was true that she *delighted in* (greatly enjoyed) *a bad guy's black humour* (making jokes about sad or terrible things) and *a tough* (strong, not emotional) *broad's* (this is a slang word for 'woman' in the US) *cynicism* (negative attitude to life). The implication is that there were attorneys who *got naughty thrills socializing with hoods* but that she was not one of them because she did not go that far in her relationships with her clients.

36 D The narrator says that most of her clients wouldn't think she was *exactly a laugh a minute* (extremely amusing to spend time with) and that she wasn't *whatever their personal definition of a good time was*. Fat Mikey *wouldn't get a kick out of* (get pleasure or excitement from) the kind of things she enjoyed doing, and Melody Ann would only go shopping at Saks (presumably a store the narrator liked shopping at) in order to *knock off* (steal) something from it. Her point is that she had nothing in common with her clients and they would not wish to spend any time with her apart from the time when she was working with them on their legal cases.

PART 6 2 MARKS PER QUESTION (TOTAL 14)

37 F In the first sentence of F, the first *it* refers back to the phrase *what they're doing* in the opening paragraph, which *It* at the beginning of the second sentence in the opening paragraph also refers to. The writer continues with this point in the first sentence of the paragraph after the gap. *So* refers back to the quote in F and is followed by what the writer believes to be the result of what Sir Peter Medawar.

38 D In D *For example* links the paragraph before the gap with the example of Robert Wilson, who the writer believes was 'wearing blinkers' and not seeing his work 'in its proper perspective'. In the paragraph after the gap, having made the point that scientists can become too absorbed in their work and not relate it to other people, the writer says that personally he wants his work to be of interest to non-specialists rather than only a few other academics.

39 **H** At the start of H, *Such a possibility* refers back to the possibility of someone 'converting an arcane paper' into something inspiring for other people, mentioned at the end of the paragraph before the gap. At the start of the paragraph after the gap, *On such occasions* refers back to the writer's talks mentioned at the end of H and means 'when I am giving talks'.

40 **A** In the first sentence of A, *them* refers back to the science reporters mentioned in the last sentence of the paragraph before the gap. The writer says that a problem they face is over-sensational (exaggerated in order to surprise and attract attention) claims on the part of scientific researchers. In the paragraph after the gap, the writer moves on to a new aspect of his subject – the lack of coverage (the extent to which something is present or discussed) that science gets in newspapers.

41 **E** In the first sentence of E, *More surprising* refers back to the success of the book mentioned at the end of the paragraph before the gap. The writers says that the success of the book he mentions in E was more surprising than the success of the other book, and he then describes the second book. In the paragraph after the gap *Nevertheless* refers back to what he says about the second book at the end of E.

42 **G** At the beginning of G, *This* refers back to the 'depressing' fact he describes at the end of the paragraph before the gap, of certain scientific matters being given more publicity than others he regards as 'more genuine'. In the paragraph after the gap, the writer moves on to another aspect of the subject – the characteristics of most scientists.

43 **C** In the first sentence of C, *have been treated as such* refers back to what he says about certain scientists in the paragraph before the gap, and means 'have been treated as eccentrics'. He then gives examples of two scientists who fit into this category. In the final paragraph, the writer moves on to another aspect of the subject and talks about the topic of science writing from the point of view of people who may be considering entering the competition.

44 **D** The writer says that in *Socrates' day*, there were *personal rivalries and grudges* (people remaining angry with each other because of actions they felt were intentionally unpleasant to them). There was *backbiting* (people secretly saying unpleasant things about others) and *cliquery* (people forming small groups to protect their own interests to the disadvantage of others).

45 **B** The writer says that Socrates' statement 'the unexamined life is not worth living' is *a central tenet for modern times* (one of the main principles of modern life) and that his philosophies are *remarkably relevant today*, because they deal with issues such as the *pursuit of happiness*, which the writer says are major issues in the West today. His ideas *are more illuminating, more necessary than ever*.

46 **E** According to the writer, Socrates was a *scapegoat* (a person blamed individually for something that was not their personal responsibility). When Athens was defeated and democracy was voted out of existence, the people of Athens *needed someone to blame* and they chose him – because of his fame and reputation, he was *a good target* for this blame.

47 **A** The writer says that Socrates *wrote not a single word down*, did not leave a *personal archive*. There is no evidence of what he was like that can be studied and so he seems *aloof* (a distant figure) and *nebulous* (unclear, mysterious).

48 **C** The writer says that she has *spent 10 years investigating the eastern Mediterranean landscape to find clues of his life and the 'Golden Age of Athens'*. To find out about him and his world, she has used *the latest archaeology, newly discovered historical sources, and the accounts of his key followers*.

49 **C** The writer says that Socrates is considered to be a *remote, tunic-clad beardy who wandered around classical columns* (a man who went around classical Athens without talking to others and who was not involved in normal life) but in fact he was *a man of the streets* who lived a busy and active life involving parties and physical training.

50 **B** Socrates *berated his peers for a selfish pursuit of material gain* – very strongly criticized his contemporaries for their desire to acquire material things, such as money and goods.

51 **A** The writer felt her *smile fade* (she became depressed) when she realized that the author she spoke to was right when he described Socrates as *a doughnut subject* – very interesting but

with a great hole in the middle where the central character should be. *She realized how hard it would be to find out about what Socrates was like as a man.*

52 **E** The writer says that Socrates was a *High-profile* figure when he was alive – well-known and receiving a lot of attention.

53 **B** The writer says that Socrates carried out a *forensic* (looking extremely carefully at every small detail) investigation of happiness and *how to lead 'the good life'*.

Writing

MARK SCHEMES
MARKS OUT OF 20 FOR EACH QUESTION
ASSESSMENT CRITERIA ARE ON PAGE 92.

QUESTION 1

Content
The essay should include a summary of these four key points:
Text 1 (a) concept of human nature is a complex and important issue
   (b) major question is whether people are naturally selfish or unselfish
Text 2 (a) human nature a philosophical rather than scientific issue
   (b) studies of human nature also involve other subjects, not only philosophy

Communicative Achievement
This is an essay and so the register should be neutral or formal. The reader should be clear both as to what the key points in each text are and the candidate's own opinions and responses to those points.

Organization
The essay should be coherently organized in paragraphs, with clear linking between the summaries of the key points and the candidate's own views. An introduction and conclusion are not essential.

Language
The essay should contain an appropriate level of accurate grammar and vocabulary. Vocabulary connected with the topics of personal characteristics and society should be correctly used, as should grammatical structures for describing and comparing points of view/information, presenting and supporting opinions, and linking points in complex sentences.

QUESTION 2

Content
Review should inform the reader as to the exact nature of the attraction, together with the writer's opinion of it.

Communicative Achievement
Register could be formal, informal or neutral but should be consistent throughout. Review format – clear paragraphing dealing with different aspects of the topic. Reader would have a clear picture of what the attraction is and has to offer, together with a clear understanding of the writer's opinions on it and whether the writer considers it worth visiting or not.

Organization
Paragraphs should each describe aspects of the attraction, in narrative form if a visit is being described, with appropriately linked comments on these aspects.

Language
Language of description, narration and evaluation.

QUESTION 3

Content
Letter should cover the points raised in the newspaper article – young people spending their time watching TV and playing computer games rather than being active or reading – and give views on this issue.

Communicative Achievement
Register appropriate for a reader writing to a newspaper on a serious matter – fairly formal. Standard letter format. Candidates can support the views expressed in the article or oppose them, or they may support some and oppose others. Reader would understand the writer's views fully and clearly.

Organization
Brief introduction, stating why the person is writing the letter. Clear organization of points with appropriate paragraphing. Perhaps brief conclusion. Appropriate linking both between and within paragraphs.

Language
Language for expressing and supporting opinions, and perhaps for making suggestions.
FOR A SAMPLE ANSWER AND ASSESSMENT OF IT, SEE PAGE 129.

QUESTION 4

Content
Article should describe the person chosen and explain why they deserve to be regarded as a hero.

Communicative Achievement
Register could be informal, formal or neutral, depending on seriousness of subject matter, but should be consistent throughout. Article format – clearly divided paragraphs, perhaps short ones for impact and perhaps sub-headings. Reader would have a clear image of the

person described and understand fully why that person is considered worthy of recognition.

Organization

Paragraphs should effectively link clear explanation of claims being made for the person and justification for them.

Language

Language of description, narration (if a particular incident is being described), together with language appropriate for expressing and supporting views.

Listening

PART 1 1 MARK PER QUESTION (TOTAL 6)

1 **B** The speaker says that the museum *is dedicated to* (its efforts have as their purpose) *ensuring that the dragonfly survives and thrives* (exists in large quantities and in good condition as a species). In its brochure people are told they *shouldn't sit back clutching our eco-guilt* (take no action but simply hold on to their feeling of guilt about what is happening to the environment) because *there are things we can do*. In other words, they are encouraged to join together with the museum and take action to protect dragonflies, which are *in danger of becoming extinct* as a result of *us and our pollution*.

2 **A** If a person 'sulks', they become silent because they are angry or offended. The speaker says that dragonflies *sulk*, for example when the weather is overcast (cloudy), which they don't like because they refuse to fly then. Since humans sulk and the speaker says that dragonflies do too, he is implying that they have the same kind of moods that people have.

3 **A** The presenter says that *there is no doubt that the Water Talkie was Richie's idea and that adult toy-makers testify* (give evidence why something should be believed) *that he has a gift for* (a talent for producing) *new ideas*. She is implying here that some people may doubt that it really was his idea and not the idea of an adult, and saying that there are toy-makers who can give good reasons why such doubts are unjustified.

4 **C** The presenter says that Richie thought that the *snag* (problem) with the toy was that the wires and batteries would get wet. Richie says that his grandfather was a *big navy guy* (someone important in the navy and therefore knowledgeable about such things), and so he and his Dad asked the grandfather to help them solve this problem. The grandfather *put us on to* (informed us of the existence of) *sonar underwater acoustics* (a technical term concerning

sound under water), and they discovered from this that sound works better underwater. The grandfather therefore played a key role in the development of the toy, and if he hadn't told them about sonar underwater acoustics, they might not have been able to develop the toy into something that could be sold.

5 **C** The speaker says that her book tries to be a work of *evocation* (communicating images and feelings that create a strong impression for others), and in this way is similar to a work of fiction, since novels also try to portray *a world, a series of values, aspirations, emotions*. She says that cookbooks which are *more picture-led* (dominated by illustrations) *and less word-driven* (do not have words as their main feature) than hers also try to do this. She is therefore saying that her book has fewer pictures and more words in it than other cookbooks.

6 **A** The speaker says that the *cookbook obsession* (people's strong desire to have cookbooks) is a result of the *disparity* between real life and life as shown in cookbooks. People don't really lead *domestic lives* (lives at home) any more, they live their lives at work and this has made their desires *turn to the home* (not having home lives has made them want to have home lives). That is why there is such a *proliferation of* (enormous increase in the number of) cookbooks – *words have to make up for the shortfall in deeds* (people need to read about doing things at home to compensate for the fact that they are not actually doing them). She says that people shouldn't *be fooled by* (get a false impression from) *cookbook consumption* (the number of cookbooks that people buy) – people read about cooking instead of doing it and *we are talking* (the situation is one of) *vicarious gratification* (getting pleasure from something other people do, rather than from something you do yourself) here. Her point is that there are so many cookbooks because people buy them so that they can read about cooking and therefore compensate for the fact that they don't actually cook themselves.

PART 2 1 MARK PER QUESTION (TOTAL 9)

7 **total sensory design**

This term means 'design that relates to all of the physical senses' and he is saying that designers nowadays have to focus not only on things like value and service, which are always important, but also on other things that shoppers may be aware of, such as the quality of the air, the amount and nature of the light and the materials used in shopping centres.

8 roundabouts

David has discovered that women find it stressful if they have to drive round a lot of roundabouts.

9 shiny surfaces

David says that flooring materials are especially important and that for them shiny surfaces are *out* (in this context, this means 'not acceptable' or 'not to be considered'), because they can be *slippery* (difficult to walk on without accidentally sliding) and make people worried that they might fall on them.

10 stone; wood

David says that people admire plastic and steel but that they *develop relationships with stone and wood*, by which he means that the latter appeal to their emotions, whereas the former do not.

11 People Like Us/PLUs

David thinks that people like to shop with *like-minded people* (people with similar tastes, opinions and attitudes). He has invented this term to describe groups of shoppers who share similar tastes, opinions and attitudes.

12 exclusive; discount

In this case, a *mall* is a section of a shopping centre (often it refers to a whole shopping centre). We can assume that the *exclusive mall* contains expensive shops for people with a lot of money ('exclusive' can mean 'limited to certain people only' and 'too expensive for most people to afford'), and that the *discount mall* contains shops selling cheaper goods.

13 Home Comfortables

This category is for *pensioners* (retired people) and *people who have stopped competing in their careers*.

14 Budget Optimists

This category is for people who *don't have huge spending power* (can't afford to spend much money) but *always think they're going to find a bargain*.

15 Young Survivors

This category is for couples who have just got married, *with one income* (only one of them works) and *just about getting by* (only just managing to survive financially, having only just enough money to live and no extra money).

PART 3 1 MARK PER QUESTION (TOTAL 5)

16 C The presenter says that almost every British paper has its star *interviewer* (this probably means both 'person who interviews stars' and 'interviewer who is a star'), and that the *bylines* (the line at the beginning or end of an article saying who the writer is) *are big and the space* (amount of space in the paper given to interviews by such people) *generous*. In other words, he is saying that the names of these interviewers are clearly seen and emphasized in papers and their articles are long ones treated as important in papers.

17 A She says that she starts by comparing things that interviewees have previously said, for example by pointing out that they said one thing in an interview in 1996 and something different in an interview in 1998. The use of 'whereas' indicates that the two things the interviewee said were not consistent with each other. The informal phrase *blah, blah, blah* is used instead of quoting something considered uninteresting that someone said and means 'etc., etc., etc.'.

18 D She says that she sends them other interviews she has written before she interviews them so that they can see *what they're in for* (the unpleasant experience they are going to have), *what they can expect*. She then expects them to *play the game* (to do what is fair in terms of what all those involved expect). Her point is that if they agree to be interviewed by her after they have seen the sort of things she writes, she thinks they should know what to expect when she interviews them and behave accordingly.

19 B She says that *a great many interviewees mistake intimacy* (close personal contact) *for real friendship* and that there is *reciprocal* (given and received in return) *warmth* (friendliness), *which can be very embarrassing*. She says that when she is doing an *ordinary human interest story* (one concerning something that has happened to an ordinary person rather than a celebrity), her *sympathy will stop the moment the interview is over*, which makes her *feel guilty* because the people she has interviewed *don't realize that*. Her point is that people she interviews think that she really becomes a friend of theirs whereas in fact she only likes them during the time when she is interviewing them and forgets all about them afterwards, and she feels embarrassed and guilty about this.

20 D He says that he tends to *protect people from themselves* (prevent them from doing harm to themselves) because sometimes they *don't realize what they say, how things might hurt their children*. He therefore implies that he might change or leave out things people say because they sometimes don't know what they are saying or the effect that what they are saying will have, and don't realize that things they say might upset their children.

PART 4 1 MARK PER QUESTION (TOTAL 10)

21 **B** The speaker says that the person (James) *stands by his friends* (supports them at all times) and that if you are his friend, he will always remain a friend of yours. He is *a friend for life*, regardless of what people who are his friends do or what people say about them.

22 **E** The speaker says that this person (Alex) *takes it in her stride* (remains calm and adapts) *whatever happens*. She *doesn't expect things to go her way* (be favourable to her) all the time and she does *whatever she has to do in the circumstances* whenever there are changes or problems.

23 **D** The speaker says that this person (Tammy) is *sharp*, notices everything and *can see right through people* – understands instinctively what people are really like. She *gets straight to the heart of the matter* – finds the truth regarding a situation or issue.

24 **G** The speaker says that the person (Jessie) *just carries on believing in herself* even though she makes some *very public mistakes*. Although some people laugh at her and think she is *a bit of a fool*, she never doubts *for a minute that what she's doing is the right thing*. The speaker says this is *the great thing about her* – her best characteristic.

25 **H** The speaker says that this person (Chris) *never gives up* and keeps trying to achieve what he wants to achieve despite any lack of progress of setbacks. He *never knows when he's beaten* – he keeps trying to succeed even when it seems unlikely that he will be able to.

26 **E** The speaker says that the person often *comes out with* (suddenly says) things that are *offensive and personally insulting*. He is not *tactful* (careful to avoid saying things that might upset people) and he says *what's on his mind* even if people might think that this is rude.

27 **C** The speaker says that there are *lots of issues* that she doesn't discuss with the person because she has *very fixed opinions* and refuses to *listen to any alternative point of view* – she is narrow-minded in connection with these particular issues.

28 **F** The speaker says that this person doesn't talk much and is not *outgoing*. She lets other people *lead the conversation* rather than speaking herself. She is a quiet person and *holds back* (doesn't speak or say what she thinks).

29 **G** The speaker says that this person tends to *have tantrums* – get angry and shout like a small child – when things don't happen in the way she wants them to happen. She says this behaviour is *just plain embarrassing for someone of her age* – for someone who is not a small child.

30 **D** The speaker says that this person *never makes allowances for other people's weaknesses* – does not tolerate them – and he *has no time for people who complain about their problems* – has no sympathy with them.

Writing sample answers

TEST 1 QUESTION 1 PART 1 ESSAY

Unsustainable and sustainable tourism

The author of the first text points out the damaging effects of unsustainable tourism. The text states how undeveloped villages have been forced to replace traditional crafts and fishing for more appealing entertainment to the tourist point of view. The statement 'Been there, Done that' results in an arrogant approach to the so valued culture of people living in the villages. Seas contaminated by sewage, vastly reduced wildlife, constant litter and air polluted by traffic are the main concerns when it comes to unsustainable tourism. The author of the second text talks about holiday spots where the damage hasn't been visible or hasn't occurred at all, and those places have been reformed and better equipped to welcome tourists. Unfortunately in most cases reforming came after the damage has been done. Reforming in holiday spots has happened mostly for public relations purposes and not to commit to sustainable tourism. With human curiosity and tourist hunger to discover new holiday places, unsustainable tourism will always cause problems for places newly open to tourism. The general need for holidays is growing vastly, and the costs of holidays abroad are sometimes cheaper than holidays people can take in own countries. As most tourists are involved in unsustainable tourism, the damage done to places and local people will continue to happen and to spread. However, a genuine commitment to sustainable tourism would bring benefits to the freshly discovered holiday spots in the long term.

Content

The two main points from the first text are included in the first paragraph of this answer. The first key point of the second text is not specifically mentioned but the second one is present, although there is some copying of the phrasing used in the text.

Communicative Achievement

The register is suitably neutral/formal. The answer fully addresses the general issues raised in both texts in a coherent way and the candidate's own views are clearly expressed in the last paragraph.

Organization

The essay is very well organised. It is divided into clear paragraphs, each having a different focus – the first text, the second text and the writer's opinions on the issues raised in the two texts. The essay flows well, with coherent linking of points in the answer as a whole and within paragraphs.

Language

The language used in the essay shows a good level of fluency. Complex sentences are used throughout and these are well constructed in terms of grammatical accuracy. The variety of noun phrases listed in the last sentence of the first paragraph is very effective, the passive is appropriately used throughout, and there is good use of the linking words *With*, *As* and *However* in the last paragraph. A range of vocabulary connected with tourism is used appropriately and the general level of vocabulary, both individual words (e.g. *arrogant, visible, occurred, curiosity, hunger*) and phrases (e.g. *vastly reduced, when it comes to, bring benefits to, in the long term*) is good. There are a couple of mistakes with prepositions in the first paragraph: *replace ... for* should be *replace .... with* and *to the tourist point of view* should be *from the tourist point of view*. In the last paragraph, own countries should be their own countries.

Mark

Despite some repetition of the second text, the essay does what is required for the task with a good level of English and few mistakes.
Band 4

TEST 1 QUESTION 4 PART 2 REVIEW

I bet that when they first made 'Friends', the producers wouldn't have expected and dreamt that their new 'attempt to amuse' bored viewers – and with totally unknown actors 'from nowhere' – would earn such a great success. After many years of living a daily life with characters from Dallas, Baywatch, Dynasty, a new wave of funny, clever and witty entertainment struck people in. And obviously, people welcomed the change very warmly. 'Friends' was full of diversity. Each of the main five characters was completely different and brought to the series something new. Despite their differences, they created a perfect working jigsaw. They lived, laughed, cried and shared their fate together. You could feel some kind of oneness there; and that is a vital thing in every friendship. Chandler – a sexist who couldn't live without women – with his ironic and sharp, witty humour, contrasted with naive, a little bit dumb but cute Joey, who had a vanity and irresistible smile in the role of an unsuccessful actor. Monica was a nagging perfectionist who often quarrelled with frivolous and untidy Rachel. Ross was a worried paleontologist who tried to come to terms that his wife left him. Poor guy! And at last weird Pheobe, who refreshed almost every episode with her 'fabulous' music which nobody could get. Oh yeah, she's quite odd but everybody loves her.

'Friends' was a great refreshment after a long, exhausting day at work. It is no wonder that it was so popular. People just loved it – from children to adults and older people as well. We need to laugh and relax. The actors, producers and creators deserve appreciation and admiration for making such a great show. People were waiting eagerly for new episodes all the time. And that's a sign of success. Not to mention that 'friends' was popular in every continent of the world. And that proves something.

Content
The review fully covers the requirements of the question, providing a detailed description of the chosen programme and a clear explanation of its popularity.

Range
There is a great deal of excellent use of sophisticated vocabulary and structure, for example, *welcomed warmly* (first paragraph), *diversity, fate, oneness* and the enormous number of adjectives used to describe people and personalities in the second paragraph, *no wonder, deserve appreciation and admiration, waiting eagerly,* and *Not to mention* (third paragraph) . The second paragraph is particularly effective.

Accuracy
There are a couple of minor errors. The phrase *struck people in* (first paragraph) does not exist and something like *came to people's attention* would be appropriate. In the second paragraph *come to terms that* should be *come to terms with the fact that* because the phrase is 'come to terms with something'. In the second paragraph, *at last* should be *finally*.

Appropriacy of Register and Format
The register is appropriately informal and the format, with its clear paragraphing, appropriate for a review.

Organization and Cohesion
The review is very well-organized. It begins by talking about the success of the programme chosen, the second paragraph provides a detailed description of the characters, and the last paragraph talks about how it deserved its success. There is good linking throughout, enabling the review as a whole to flow very well.

Target Reader
The reader would be absolutely clear as to what the series was like, why it was popular and why the writer liked it so much.

Mark
An excellent and virtually fluent review, with a lot of very good and appropriate vocabulary.
Band 5

TEST 2 QUESTION 2 PART 2 REPORT
REPORT – SOCIAL PROBLEMS
I think that the programme should focus on these three main areas:
CRIME
Crime is a big problem that has been rising in recent times. There has been a big increase in the number of burglaries and also in muggings on the street. Some people seem to think that, if they haven't got as much in life as they want, they can just take it from somebody else. As a result, a lot of ordinary people are fearful and a lot of victims of these crimes are permanently affected.

YOUTH PROBLEMS
A lot of youngsters seem to feel bored, alienated from society or cynical about life. This leads some of them to turn to crime, for example in the form of hooliganism. Vandalism is widespread and we can observe the results of that in many places. Besides causing a lot of damage, this makes a lot of people worried about the future of society. The only way to turn this situation around is to try to prevent these young people to continue to have such negative attitudes by showing them how they can make a positive contribution to society. They need to realise that doing so will make them feel better about themselves.
UNEMPLOYMENT
Whether it's because of inadequate education or just unfortunate circumstances, unemployment leads to several problems, such as debts, depression, crime, etc. Unemployment creates a tense and agitated home environment. This affects children in a most destructive way. Children need to feel safe. Their schoolwork and social development will suffer.

Content
The report fully covers the areas required in the question, since it lists three social problems and discusses both the causes and the consequences of them.

Range
There is some good use of vocabulary and structure, for example *rising steadily, burglaries, muggings* and *fearful* (first section), *alienated from, cynical about, turn to, Besides causing, turn this situation around,* and *make a positive contribution to* (second section) and the use of Whether for linking, *tense, agitated* and *destructive* (third section).

Accuracy
There is only one error. In the second section *prevent these young people to continue* should be *prevent these young people from continuing*.

Appropriacy of Register and Format
The register is appropriately neutral and the format is entirely appropriate, with a heading for the report and three clear sections with clear headings.

Organization and Cohesion
The report is very well-organized, with each section providing a clear description of each problem and a brief analysis of its causes and consequences. The linking is accurate and appropriate.

Target Reader
The reader would be completely clear as to the points made by the writer.

Mark
A clear, accurate and competent report.
Band 4

TEST 3 QUESTION 4 PART 2 ARTICLE

It is said that dreaming is a wonderful thing. But much better – of course – when our dreams do not stay just wishes, but when they come true. Well, some people, realizing what it possibly could cost them, give up at the very beginning and remain in that sweet state of consciousness trying to escape from reality.

I suppose I've always been a tough cookie since my early childhood. Poor Mum. She was really happy when I gave up the idea of being an electrician and found my passion for art but I found later that it wasn't the thing I had been looking for. Something was still missing. And suddenly, like a spark of fire, I realized what it was – music. I fell in love with my uncle's piano. His job was to repair and tune the pianos. My parents took no notice of my suggestion to buy one for me. My mum icily said: 'No way. I know you. It would be like with your 'famous' painting. You'll give up after a while. All the stuff I bought for you is left in the corner in your room. It cost me a fortune. And by the way, your fingers are too short for playing. Did I make myself clear?' I had a proper look at my fingers. I wanted to cry. She was right.

I was really stubborn. I pretended that my interest in possibly being a famous piano player had left me but … . I took up lessons after my school finished in the afternoon; passionately learnt the notes and slowly discovered the secrets of keys, tones and chords. My passion grew more day by day and kept me continuing. A friend of mine put her piano at my disposal for I didn't have any at home and I could go to my uncle's house just occasionally. We used to play and learn together. Her parents were great. I used to say at home that we had had some games like football (trustworthy enough for Mum) and basketball after school to keep us fit and have some kind of interests – not just TV. My 'little secret' was revealed when my Mum discovered my exercise book. She lost her tongue and couldn't believe her eyes. And later even her ears. I was rather happy and immediately suggested: 'So now that YOU KNOW (I emphasized) you can buy me a piano.' But she needed proof of my ability. I was forced to go to my uncle's house and play for her. She was amazed. This happened two weeks before my birthday. I kept playing behind her back almost for two years. Quite stubborn, hm? On my birthday we had a performance in the local theatre. I felt so happy. My parents sat among the other parents waiting to see their beloved child performing on the stage. The concert itself was a great success. I played Beethoven's Moonlight Sonata. My parents were so proud of me and couldn't stop clapping at the end. When we returned home, a surprise waited for me in my room: a brand-new polished piano. Tears appeared on my face. I remember kissing and stroking it like a pet.

I persisted in spite of the stubborn attitude of my parents and achieved what I had been dreaming of. And today, I just smile at these memories while playing on my own piano. A strong passion can make miracles.

Content

The article fully covers everything mentioned in the question – it is entirely suited to the title, it describes the writer's aim, details what the writer did to achieve it and includes the writer's general view about taking risks in life.

Range

The language used is very sophisticated, with some excellent use of vocabulary and structure, for example *come true*, the participle clause beginning *realizing and remain in that sweet state of consciousness* (first paragraph), *tough cookie, like a spark of fire, icily, cost me a fortune* and *Did I make myself clear?* (second paragraph), *stubborn, day by day* and *put her piano at my disposal* (third paragraph), *behind her back, beloved* and *stroking it like a pet* (fourth paragraph) and *persisted* and *dreaming of* (final paragraph).

Accuracy

There are one or two mistakes. In the last sentence of the third paragraph, *trustworthy* should be something like 'believable', since 'trustworthy' usually decribes a person. In the fourth paragraph, *She lost her tongue* should be *She was speechless* and *I kept playing* should be *I had kept playing*, since this refers to the period before the episode at her uncle's house, not something she did after that.

Appropriacy of Register and Format

The register here is fairly informal, and this is entirely appropriate for an article that is about the writer's personal experience and contains anecdotes. The style is lively and engaging, with some short sentences aimed at having impact on the reader, some direct speech and a rhetorical question aimed directly at the reader (*Quite stubborn, hm?*) – these features are particularly suited to the style and format of an article.

Organization and Cohesion

The article is extremely well-organized. The brief opening paragraph presents a general statement that the rest of the article is clearly going to illustrate. The second paragraph begins the narration with the background, the third paragraph describes a long period in which the writer tried to achieve her aim and the fourth paragraph moves on to the outcome of all this. In the last part of the article, the writer looks back on the whole experience and the final sentence links back to the attitude expressed in the opening paragraph. Everything is linked together well, so that the narration of events moves on logically and at a good pace.

Target Reader

The reader would have no trouble at all in understanding what the writer wanted to achieve, how she went about achieving it, how she finally achieved it and how she felt and feels about it all. The writer's enthusiasm is clearly conveyed in an article which fulfils entirely the instructions given in the question.

Mark
An excellent, virtually fluent and highly effective article with sophisticated language. The article is much longer than the word limit specified for Part 2, but candidates are not penalised for exceeding the word limit.
Band 5

TEST 4 QUESTION 3 PART 2 LETTER

Dear Editorial Staff,

I've read your article about young people very thoroughly and can't deny the truth of most facts you give, but what I really dislike is how you blame our children for that.

It is true that children of today don't play football in the streets any more to get rid of all their energy or meet outside to play with marbles, nowadays it is more likely to find them sitting in front of the computer or the television. But consider the circumstances: 'It's much too dangerous to play outside,' most of the parents sensibly decide. However children need to play. Lucky the one's that have neighbour's that can come over whenever they like. But that case is very rare and mostly the parents haven't got time to play with the children. TV and the computer is the best way to keep them occupied and quiet. And here begins the vicious circle. The TV and computer games present to children the heart of materialism and imaginary worlds which are not only one child's but they can discuss them with their friends at school. The ones who read books or have only their own imaginations are 'out', they don't belong to the multi-media children's group. This mechanism makes all children long for more and always the latest games, videos, etc. And it spoils all efforts of the few parents that try to bring up their children without TV and computer games.

By the way many children read books as well, but that is not what rules their lives, they don't get attention for that mostly. An exception is shown by J.K. Rowling and her 'Harry Potter' books. Maybe she found the key to even the multi-media children's mind through a book, at least she made everyone read – until the Harry Potter books were read on tape, and then made in to films. That shows how our society forces everything to fit in the multi-media complex and that everybody's minds, especially the children's, are surrendered to it almost helplessly. The frightening thing is that most people don't realise what generations of scientific and economic progress have created and what that leads to.

Your article may have helped at least to show some of that even though you blamed the wrong ones. It's everybody's fault.

Yours faithfully,

Content
The letter covers all the issues raised in the article and is directly relevant to them throughout. The writer has mainly agreed with the main point of the article and given reasons in support of it and explanations of causes for it. The writer has also pointed out an exception to the main point.

Range
There is good use of vocabulary and structure, for example *can't deny the truth of* (first paragraph), *get rid of, sensibly decide, vicious circle, 'out', long for* and *the few parents* (second paragraph), and *found the key to* and *are surrendered to it almost helplessly* (third paragraph). The sentences are not only short and simple and much of the language used for presenting the argument is quite sophisticated.

Accuracy
There are a couple of mistakes. In the first sentence of the second paragraph *it is more likely to find*, should be *you are more likely to find* or *it is more likely that you will find*, since 'find' needs a subject. In the fourth sentence of the second paragraph, there should not be apostrophes in one's and neighbour's, since these are not being used possessively. These mistakes do not affect understanding.

Appropriacy of Register and Format
The register is entirely appropriate and a serious and fairly complex set of points is expressed in a fairly formal tone. The format is fine.

Organization and Cohesion
The letter is very well-organized. The brief introductory paragraph sets out both the reason for writing and the writer's general point of view, the second paragraph both supports the view and gives a number of reasons why the situation described has come about, the third paragraph begins with an exception to the general point but then skilfully links it back to that general point, and the final paragraph concisely and forcefully sums up the writer's view, linking it once again to the article being responded to. There is some good linking, for example *But consider* (second paragraph), *at least* (third and final paragraph) and *even though* (final paragraph). Much of the linking is relatively simple ('And' and 'But') but this does not spoil the letter or badly affect the way it flows.

Target Reader
The reader would fully understand the writer's views and the general point – that what is said in the article is true but that it is not the fault of young people themselves – is forcefully made. The letter generally flows well and logically.

Mark
A very good letter that makes its points forcefully.
Band 4

AUDIO SCRIPTS

TEST 1

Cambridge Certificate of Proficiency in English Listening Test. Test 1. I'm going to give you the instructions for this test. I'll introduce each part of the test and give you time to look at the questions. At the start of each piece you'll hear this sound:
TONE
You'll hear each piece twice.
Remember, while you're listening, write your answers on the question paper. You'll have five minutes at the end of the test to copy your answers onto the separate answer sheet. There will now be a pause. Please ask any questions now, because you must not speak during the test.
PAUSE 5 seconds
Now open your question paper and look at Part 1.
PAUSE 5 seconds

(PART ONE)

You will hear three different extracts. For questions **1–6**, choose the answer (**A**, **B** or **C**) which fits best according to what you hear. There are two questions for each extract.

Extract One
PAUSE 15 seconds
TONE

Man: 'The Two Cultures'; what an alluring little phrase that is. Everyone has an opinion about it, but no one knows what it means – beyond the vague idea that the arts and science are worryingly separate and at loggerheads. When National Science Week begins on Friday, scientists will be trying to persuade us that science is just as important as the arts in British national culture. Are they right – or is science just a narrow specialism, increasingly in need of self-promotion? The term 'The Two Cultures' was coined by the late C P Snow, who distinguished himself not so much by attempting to work in both the arts and science, as by achieving nothing in either of them. As well as writing numerous unspeakable novels, he had a scientific career whose highlight was a well-publicized claim to have manufactured artificial vitamin A, a finding other scientists swiftly discredited. Yet only a churl would deny that he struck a chord with his 1959 lecture, when he claimed that western intellectual life 'is increasingly being split into two polar groups'. At one pole were the literary intellectuals, at the other the physical scientists.
PAUSE 5 seconds
TONE
REPEAT Extract One
PAUSE 2 seconds

Extract Two
PAUSE 15 seconds
TONE

Woman: We did an exercise on ticketing five years ago and discovered that 400 tickets were lost by clients every year before they'd even left the UK. But the amazing thing is the reasons – all genuine. The dog ate them, the baby threw them in the fire, the wife tore them up in a rage; that's quite apart from all the ones you'd expect, such as they were in the car and the car got stolen. If losses were going at the same ratio today, with the increase in our business, that would mean three a day. One of my favourite stories is about a chap we were taking to the US for very serious heart surgery. The hospital was near Rochester, so they booked him to Rochester, New York. When this chap got out, picked his bag up and went to a taxi driver and asked, 'How far to this hospital?', the cabbie replied, 'About 1,500 miles.' He was meant to go to Rochester, Minnesota. The nice part of the story is that United Airlines, who had flown him transatlantic, understood his plight and got him on the next flight to Rochester, Minnesota, no charge. The reason we know the story is not because he came back to us ranting and raving, but because he saw the funny side of it.
PAUSE 5 seconds
TONE
REPEAT Extract Two
PAUSE 2 seconds

Extract Three
PAUSE 15 seconds
TONE

Reporter: Victoria and Mark's son Freddie is now nearly five and being with his parents on location appears to have done him no harm at all. Out in the bush, his crèche has included baby hippos and pythons. In fact, says Victoria, Freddie's known as 'Snakeboy'.
Victoria: That's because he's always picking them up, and walking about with them round his neck. We moved to a new location where some of the snakes were deadly, so we told him that he must call somebody before he touched a snake. So then he walked around shouting 'Somebody! Somebody!'
Reporter: Their current location looks rather exotic on film. Mark, however, is quick to dispel any notions of tasting paradise.
Mark: We live in these coconut and mangrove huts. If it's really raining, we close all the coconut leaves and it feels like you're in a wicker basket. Just before we left to come on this trip to England, it was raining so much the verandah fell down. Apart from mudslides, we've no running water. We have to go by donkey to collect water from the well. And the sleeping arrangements are very primitive. Three to a small hut. Privacy is very much a luxury of the Western World.
PAUSE 5 seconds
TONE
REPEAT Extract Three
PAUSE 2 seconds

That's the end of Part 1. Now turn to Part 2.
PAUSE 5 seconds

(PART TWO)
You will hear someone called Kate Charters describing her career. For questions 7–15, complete the sentences with a word or short phrase.
You now have forty-five seconds in which to look at Part 2.
[PAUSE THE RECORDINGS FOR 45 SECONDS]
TONE
Kate: Well, as you know, I've been invited to the college today to give you some advice on careers in sales, as you approach the end of your business courses. Most of what I've done has involved sales of one sort or another, and I thought I'd start by giving you a brief summary of my own career. My first job was with Business Traveller magazine, where I sold classified advertising over the phone. I did this for a year, coming to it from a business skills course I took. I had graduated with a degree in English, and I decided I'd better have some basic skills before throwing myself on the marketplace. So I did all the things I said I'd never do, like learning to type and do shorthand, and so on.
Three years after that, having done various other sales jobs, I became a marketing co-ordinator with Soundcraft Electronics. We made sound-mixing equipment for recording studios. This was a terrific job. I started as assistant to the chairman, and I basically created my own job, which involved dealing with the advertising and promotional side, too. Then I joined the company I now work for, Visnews. It is a major global television newsgathering organization, based in London, with branches all over the world. I joined as a marketing executive in their film library. We have a huge archive of videotape and newsreel films going back to the very beginning of motion pictures. My job was to increase revenues from the archive through usage fees. After a short while I helped to start a new department which was producing and selling videos for the retail market – what we call 'sell-through' programming. These would be documentaries that people would buy, so they would usually have a special-interest theme ... and, of course, they'd make extensive use of our archives. Visnews Video eventually had 11 titles which we sold at retail outlets and through direct marketing techniques. I was headhunted away from this to join Castle Communications, where my job was to sell feature films on video to the rental and sell-through markets. My job was to come up with ways to inspire our salesforce to move the merchandise. I was also responsible for developing side deals. One time we worked a deal with a major theme park, where we used the venue for a launch event, and carried a promotion for the park on the front of the video. Meanwhile, the park cross-promoted the video on site. I was with Castle for a year, then I rejoined Visnews as a sales co-ordinator in the Special Locations Department, which is the operation I now head. The job involves some travel. Last week I was in Spain calling on several of our clients and building our relationships. A few months ago, I spent a week in Moscow. And what do I do? Well, I run the department that offers camera crews, editing facilities and satellite technology to broadcasters and video production companies worldwide. I have six sales co-ordinators working with me. I think as you go through your career, it's very important to have a mentor. I've been lucky to have the advice of a man who works in a PR agency I dealt with when I was first at Visnews. Over the years, just having someone to talk to as I contemplated moves or wanted to discuss career activities, has been tremendously helpful. He's always been interested in what I've been doing and very supportive. I've valued his advice most highly. OK, before we move on to ...
PAUSE 10 seconds
Now you'll hear Part 2 again.
TONE
REPEAT Part 2
PAUSE 5 seconds
That's the end of Part 2. Now turn to Part 3.
PAUSE 5 seconds

(PART THREE)
You will hear an interview with a British politician. For questions 16–20, choose the answer (A, B, C or D) which fits best according to what you hear.
You now have one minute in which to look at Part 3.
[PAUSE THE RECORDING FOR 1 MINUTE]
TONE
Interviewer: My guest today is former government minister, Susan Graham. While always regarded as somewhat unusual, it was only after her attack on her colleague Martin Jones for his policies as senior government minister responsible for prisons, that she started to attract considerable media attention, by no means all flattering, or, indeed, relevant. Susan, as a politician, do you always act on the things you believe are right?
Susan: I've always put my views on conscience issues, always, even if I know some of them are unpopular. I put them to the electorate so that people know exactly what they're getting. I think that is important. There is one thing I do despise, actually, and I really do despise it, it's the politician who tries to have things all ways, not because he says honestly, 'Actually, I haven't made my mind up,' that's different, occasionally we don't make our minds up. But the politician who says, 'Well, actually, I think this but it's a bit unpopular so I'm going to try and dress it up and I'm going to try and present it in a different way to the electorate.' That I actually think is wrong.
Interviewer: Is politics your whole life?
Susan: Certainly I do not wish to be engaged in any other

profession other than politics.

Interviewer:
So what do you say to those people who feel that in the tremendous battle with Martin Jones, your political future could well have been closed off?

Susan: Oh, that was a price that I knew that I would have to pay right from the start. I'm aware that this will be open to misinterpretation, but I felt that in a way I was being brought to the time of trial. That if I let that weigh with me, that if I let my own political future weigh with me over an issue which I did consider to be enormously important in all sorts of different ways, then really it wouldn't be worth having as a political future. As I've said, to look at self-advancement in its own right, it isn't worth a damn, it really isn't.

Interviewer: You would have got support privately, I'm sure, but in the end your colleagues didn't support you publicly, did they?

Susan: No, let me make it very clear. One or two colleagues did very kindly come out in support. I actually said to them, 'No, you know, this is something I want to do alone. It is something that it is much better that I do alone without embroiling other people in it.'

Interviewer: But isn't politics always about embroiling other people?

Susan: No, it's not always about embroiling other people.

Interviewer: Very often, then, very often.

Susan: It can often be about embroiling other people but not always, not invariably. I think there are some things about which you say, 'I don't actually want to get anybody else caught up with this. This is something which I feel I've got to do.' What I said was very straightforward: I'm going to make my doubts and my reservations known. It is then entirely up to my colleagues whether they take those into account or not, and if they want to say no, they're not going to take those into account, that's up to them. I did my duty at the point that I made my doubts and reservations known. I didn't have to go any further.

Interviewer: But doesn't it affect your judgement of your colleagues that they didn't support you publicly? You felt so strongly, this is something you said was massively important.

Susan: I think every time you take a stand on something, and I have taken a number of stands in my time, then quite obviously the way that you look at your fellow MPs is going to be somewhat coloured by whether they share that stand, whether they actively oppose that stand, whether they just shrug neutrally. It would be somewhat coloured. But politics is a great kaleidoscope of changing alliances and people that you can be bitterly opposed to one day are people with whom you can be allied the next. And therefore the fact that there were some colleagues who thought I was quite mad and there were other colleagues who gave me a lot of support but made sure

it was all extremely sotto voce, and behind closed doors, that is something that I would expect and I have no doubt that there will be other issues when some of those colleagues and I will swap positions.

Interviewer: You would expect them to think you were mad?

Susan: I would expect some of them to think I'm bonkers because I'm afraid there are some politicians who believe that you should never, ever, ever, under any circumstances, do anything to rock the boat, and you should always put yourself first and I actually went against both those two great criteria.

Interviewer: Now, to change the subject, I'd like to …

PAUSE 10 seconds

Now you'll hear Part 3 again.

TONE

REPEAT Part 3

PAUSE 5 seconds

That's the end of Part 3. Now turn to Part 4.

PAUSE 5 seconds

(PART FOUR)

Part 4 consists of two tasks. You will hear five short extracts in which people are talking about books they have read. Look at Task 1. For questions **21–25**, choose from the list (**A–H**) why each speaker read the book. Now look at Task 2. For questions **26–30**, choose from the list (**A–H**) each speaker's opinion of the book. While you listen, you must complete both tasks. You now have forty-five seconds in which to look at Part 4.

[PAUSE THE RECORDING FOR 45 SECONDS]

TONE

Speaker One

PAUSE 2 seconds

I decided it was something that I ought to know more about. I had some recollections of that period but I was very young then and I wanted to find out more about what was going on then. My parents and relatives, that generation, talked about a lot of things but I didn't really engage with it all then, I was too young. I picked it from a list I found on a website because it looked as if it wouldn't be dull. And that was right, it was lively and very accessible, and not at all dry. It made the events and changes of that period come to life.

PAUSE 3 seconds

Speaker Two

PAUSE 2 seconds

There was an enormous amount of hype about this when it came out, so I'd certainly heard all about it when I came across it in the airport bookshop. It's not the sort of thing I normally like, but there wasn't much else to choose from and I thought it would pass the journey in an easy enough way. But in fact, it wasn't the light read I was expecting. The story is very complicated, with different

narratives interwoven, and you really have to concentrate hard to follow what's going on. I had to keep going back to check things.
PAUSE 3 seconds
Speaker Three
PAUSE 2 seconds
I haven't read anything you could describe as a 'serious book' for a very long time, so I thought it was time to break that habit. I picked it out in a bookshop, mostly because of the cover, I must admit, which made it look intriguing, as did the blurb on the back. Now I've found out it's something of a surprise best-seller, acquiring a cult following despite little or no publicity – it's all been word of mouth. And I can see why. It's really quite odd and the style is very individual. Not really my sort of thing, actually, but I can see why it's taken off.
PAUSE 3 seconds
Speaker Four
PAUSE 2 seconds
Other people kept telling me how good this author is, but it never sounded like something I would enjoy. So I wasn't totally thrilled when I got given the book and put off reading it for quite some time. In the end I only read it in case she asked me what I thought of it! Well, my reservations turned out to be pretty accurate and I gave up pretty quickly. Why do people go on about how good a writer he is? It's the sort of adolescent writing anyone could come up with. How on earth this sort of stuff gets published, let alone critically acclaimed, is beyond me.
PAUSE 3 seconds
Speaker Five
PAUSE 2 seconds
I wanted to find out what all the fuss was about, whether it lives up to all the high praise it's been getting. Everything I read about it made big claims for it as a major and important work and I thought I'd better see if deserved all that. Well, I'd say on balance that it was a bit of a let-down in terms of style. However, he does have some interesting points of view to put across and they make you question your assumptions and look at the issues from a very different angle.
PAUSE 10 seconds
Now you will hear Part 4 again.
TONE
REPEAT PART 4
PAUSE 5 seconds
That's the end of Part 4.
There will now be a pause of five minutes for you to copy your answers onto the separate answer sheet. Be sure to follow the numbering of all the questions. Then your supervisor will collect all the question papers and answer sheets.

TEST 2
Cambridge Certificate of Proficiency in English Listening Test. Test 2. I'm going to give you the instructions for this test. I'll introduce each part of the test and give you time to look at the questions. At the start of each piece you'll hear this sound:
TONE
You'll hear each piece twice. Remember, while you're listening, write your answers on the question paper. You'll have five minutes at the end of the test to copy your answers onto the separate answer sheet.
There will now be a pause. Please ask any questions now, because you must not speak during the test.
PAUSE 5 seconds
Now open your question paper and look at Part 1.
PAUSE 5 seconds

(PART ONE)
You will hear three different extracts. For questions **1–6**, choose the answer (**A**, **B** or **C**) which fits best according to what you hear. There are two questions for each extract.
Extract One
PAUSE 15 seconds
TONE
Presenter: Do you freak when the car won't start? Are you tired of having to turn to your boyfriend every time the engine splutters? Then the car maintenance course for women at Bromley Adult Education Centre is a must. It promises to equip you – after one term – to carry out basic car maintenance and give your car a regular servicing. Not only will it give you independence, but it could save you a few quid too. Eighteen-year-old Helen Danks signed up after buying a cheap second-hand car.
Helen: I didn't have a clue about cars and I thought it might help if I ever broke down on the motorway. I found out that my car was rattling at speed because the tyres needed balancing. My car had always done that and I thought it was because it was old. I took it straight down the garage and told them what was wrong. The mechanic looked at me as if to say 'You don't know what you're talking about', but I explained to him about the course and he admitted he was quite impressed. And they can't rip me off now, either.
PAUSE 5 seconds
TONE
REPEAT Extract One
PAUSE 2 seconds
Extract Two
PAUSE 15 seconds
TONE
Female receptionist: Well, there are people who say, 'Oh hello, I don't think you'll be able to help me, but I suppose it's worth a try.' To this, I reply with heavy sarcasm: 'Yes,

well, we are fairly useless, but you never know. It's a long shot, but give it a whirl, we might surprise you.' Then there are people who carry on a conversation after you've answered. You start off: 'Hello, Enquiries, can I help you?' A distant voice says something like: 'And then he just left me standing there, like an idiot, with just one shoe on!' You say: 'Hello, Enquiries, CAN I HELP YOU?' They say something like: 'Well, I couldn't just leave ... oh, hello, sorry, yes ... er ... oh, I can't remember who I called now.' The polite thing to do is wait until they've got a grip. The far more satisfying thing to do is ring off just as they remember what they wanted to ask.

PAUSE 5 seconds

TONE

REPEAT Extract Two

PAUSE 2 seconds

EXTRACT THREE

PAUSE 15 seconds

TONE

Woman: Apart from good food and drink, the main requisite for a successful picnic is, of course, delightful surroundings. Some people ignore this rule completely and get out their folding tables and wrapped-up sandwiches on grotty grass verges by the side of major roads and busy car parks. It is a particularly English folly to want to eat out of doors on high days and holidays – whatever the weather. Who has not seen people in macs sitting bizarrely under dripping trees in parks, glumly handing round the flask of tea, and cheese and onion crisps? The obsessive picnic tradition probably originated in mediaeval times with pilgrims' wayside meals, as well as the gargantuan outdoor feasts held before hunting parties. By the 17th century, it was common entertainment for the gentry to eat out of doors 'in the rustic manner'. However, so worried were they that inclement weather might spoil their great hooped dresses and satin breeches, that they dotted little Arcadian pavilions around their grounds as a precautionary measure, to dive into if it rained. It was not until the 18th century that the essential picnic staple was invented by John Montagu, the fourth Earl of Sandwich ... that evocative and much-maligned British food icon that took his name.

PAUSE 5 seconds

TONE

REPEAT Extract Three

PAUSE 2 seconds

That's the end of Part 1. Now turn to Part 2.

PAUSE 5 seconds

(PART TWO)

You will hear part a radio interview with a diver. For questions **7–15**, complete the sentences with a word or short phrase. You now have forty-five seconds in which to look at Part 2.

[PAUSE THE RECORDING FOR 45 SECONDS]

TONE

Interviewer: John, how did you become interested in diving?

John: I always had a great interest in underwater adventure. When I was about 13, I experimented with a friend by converting some submarine escape apparatus we found. I tied a sack of bricks around my waist and was lowered into about 15 feet of water in the harbour. When I jerked the rope to signal that I had had enough, I saw the rope snaking down towards me. I had to haul myself up the harbour wall with the bricks weighing me down and surfaced completely blue in the face. I then joined the local sub-aqua club, the first in the British Isles, but it wasn't until I joined the Royal Engineers that I was trained properly.

Interviewer: What was so appealing?

John: It was a new frontier. In those days, people didn't go under water. Going into a different environment was a challenge – like going to the moon. Being able to move with a mere flick of a hand or foot is like flying.

Interviewer: Has the equipment changed much since you started?

John: In the Army we used modified fire-fighting apparatus. We wore cumbersome rubber drysuits over a corduroy undersuit and were completely encased. The mind boggles when you look at the advances made since then!

Interviewer: Is there anything you don't like under water?

John: I've always felt uneasy around sharks. You hear of ploys to chase them off, but if a great white is heading for you at 80 mph, you don't stand a chance. Luckily I've never been attacked by one, but some have come very close and I saw one go for a cameraman once.

Interviewer: Have you ever made any serious mistakes?

John: The worst was when I got carried away during an archaeological search off Paphos in Cyprus. I saw an ancient marble slab and was determined to bring it to the surface. As I was struggling to bring it up, I suddenly realized I was running out of air. I had to drop the slab, and surfaced too fast. I was swallowing water and I could hear rattling in my lungs. My limbs stopped working and I was being swept by a powerful current towards some jagged rocks. It was terrifying because it happened so slowly and I knew it was all my fault. Luckily a chap taking photos drew alongside in a boat, said : 'Everything all right?' and dragged me out.

Interviewer: Was that your most frightening experience?

John: I think so, although I had another bad moment while trying to raise a crane that had sunk in the mud of a harbour. Two of us were tunnelling through the mud underneath it when I felt a pressure change in my ears and realised it was sinking on top of us. We eased back through the mud, unable to see a thing, and said a few well-chosen words to each other!

Interviewer: What is the most beautiful place you have dived?

John: Roatan, which is part of Honduras. The bay is secluded and full of wrecks from aircraft to boats dating back almost to the times of Columbus. The layers of marine life go on and on into the void and the colours are more vivid than any I have seen.

Interviewer: Have you ever really hurt yourself?

John: I smashed three front teeth out while testing a human torpedo device in Florida. I hit the wrong controls by mistake and shot into the roof of a cave.

Interviewer: Have your attitudes or preferences changed?

John: I enjoy watching fish more now I've had my share of adventure. I'm also particularly interested in the conservation side. It didn't take long to realise that killing fish was a bit pointless and that if everyone did it stocks would be depleted.

Interviewer: What is the most important lesson that you have learned?

John: You can never be too careful. Familiarity breeds contempt and it's easy to forget safety checks. If you're going to learn, join a good club and learn with trained instructors. Buy the best equipment and don't dive alone. It could be your life.

Interviewer: John, thanks for talking to me today.

PAUSE 10 seconds

Now you'll hear Part 2 again.

TONE

REPEAT Part 2

PAUSE 5 seconds

That's the end of Part 2. Now turn to Part 3.

PAUSE 5 seconds

(PART THREE)

You will hear part of a radio phone-in programme about consumer competitions that appear in magazines or are run by shops, in which advice is given to people who regularly enter them. For questions **16–20**, choose the answer (**A, B, C** or **D**) which fits best according to what you hear. You now have one minute in which to look at Part 3.

[PAUSE THE RECORDING FOR 1 MINUTE]

TONE

Presenter: OK, today I have with me Kathy Ford, winner of more than £500,000 worth of prizes in all sorts of consumer competitions and dubbed 'The Queen of Competitions' by the British press. She's now editor of *Competitor's World* magazine and as an expert on competitions has appeared regularly on TV. Kathy, let's go straight to our first caller, and that's Diana. Diana, what's your query?

Diana: Yes, hello Kathy. Well, in order to send in two entries to a competition where only one entry per person was allowed, I asked my best friend if I could submit an entry in her name. She agreed, and the understanding was that, if 'her' entry won, I would receive the prize, but I would buy her a small gift for allowing me to use her name. Well, the inevitable has happened – I've won a much-needed new washing machine, but in my friend's name, and she has now refused point blank to hand the machine over. If I went to a lawyer, would I have any hope of getting my prize from her?

Kathy: Not even the faintest chance. I'm afraid that your efforts to evade the rules have not only cost you the prize, but also your best friend as well, and legally you just don't have a leg to stand on. Even if you'd drawn up some sort of legal agreement with your erstwhile friend, I think you'd find that the law would still take a very dim view of your case, since it was obviously done with premeditated fraudulent intent. It's not worth trying to evade the rules as you've just found out the hard way.

Presenter: Next, it's Ron. Ron, go ahead, you're through to Kathy.

Ron: Someone told me that some firms that run competitions keep a blacklist of frequent prizewinners, and that I should use a lot of different aliases in order to avoid being put on such a list. Is this true?

Kathy: No! Competitors can sometimes get a little paranoid, and if they start going through a winless spell (and we all get them, from time to time!) they start to imagine that they've been blacklisted. No reputable firm would even contemplate such a measure, and the only time there's even a faint risk of this sort of thing happening is with 'in store' competitions, where an individual store manager might just conceivably think 'Oh no, not him again' and deliberately disregard your entry. For mainstream competitions, however, such worries are groundless, and the use of aliases is not only unnecessary but can even prove to be pretty stupid. Think about it for a moment – what would happen if you won a holiday under a phoney name? Or were asked to prove your identity to collect a prize at a presentation ceremony? My advice is to stick with your own name and if prizes stop arriving, take a long, close look at the quality of your entries rather than trying to blame it on blacklists.

Presenter: OK, next it's Stan. Stan, what can Kathy help you with?

Stan: Well, Kathy, I recently entered a competition which asked you to estimate the distance between a store in Newcastle and its London head office, using the shortest route. In order to make my entry as accurate as possible, I used a Routemaster computer program to determine the shortest possible way and calculate the distance, quite literally, from door to door. Imagine my astonishment, therefore, when I sent for the results and found that the answer they had given as being 'correct' was fully 73 miles longer than mine. I know my answer was correct, so do I have grounds to make a formal objection?

Kathy: I'm sorry, but no, you haven't. As far as the promoter is concerned, the key word in the instructions, here, is 'estimate' – they expect you to guess, not measure the distance accurately, and it's likely that their own answer will also be based purely on an estimate. As a result, judges will always be right, even when they are wrong as in a case like this, and in entering the competition at all, you have agreed to abide by the rule that states 'the judges' decision is final'. Distance estimation competitions have always given rise to this sort of controversy, and although court cases have been brought, the entrant very seldom succeeds in having the decision changed. You have only to check the distance charts in road atlases to see how this type of problem occurs. No two ever agree, yet as far as I know, towns simply don't move around very much!

Presenter: OK, and now on to our next caller, who is …

PAUSE 10 seconds

Now you'll hear Part 3 again.

TONE

REPEAT Part 3

PAUSE 5 seconds

That's the end of Part 3. Now turn to Part 4.

PAUSE 5 seconds

(PART 4)

Part 4 consists of two tasks. You will hear five short extracts in which people are talking about their day at work. Look at Task 1. For questions **21–25**, choose from the list (**A–H**) what happened at work. Now look at Task 2. For questions **26–30**, choose from the list (**A–H**) each speaker's feeling about what happened. While you listen, you must complete both tasks. You now have forty-five seconds in which to look at Part 4.

[PAUSE THE RECORDING FOR 45 SECONDS]

TONE

Speaker One

PAUSE 2 seconds

I didn't think there was any point doing it but I had to just do as I was told and get on with it. It took me ages because it all had to be ready ahead of the meeting at the end of the day, and I slogged away without much of a break to get it all done. And guess what? They didn't have time to discuss it in the meeting, which is what I'd guessed anyway. It's the sort of thing that happens quite often but I've got used to it now. In this particular case, I think that what I did might very well prove to have been worth it eventually, because I think there's a good chance they'll go ahead with the project before too long.

PAUSE 3 seconds

Speaker Two

PAUSE 2 seconds

Well, nobody's perfect, and that includes him, so I don't know why he thinks he can tell everyone else off when he's always getting things wrong himself. There's no point arguing with him, though, you just get in even more trouble, as some of my colleagues have found out

to their cost. So I just had to take it when he came and made a big thing about how badly I'd done the work. In actual fact, the problem was a trivial one that took about 10 seconds to fix. I never let it get to me, though, I know what he's like, and it doesn't bother me.

PAUSE 3 seconds

Speaker Three

PAUSE 2 seconds

It's strange to suddenly find myself singled out. I never thought they'd choose me for the trade fair, I assumed there were far better candidates. It's the sort of thing that will stand me in very good stead and might lead to other things too. I never expected such a thing to happen and if I'm honest I'm not sure I'm ready for it. The prospect of going there and being responsible for potential deals and new business fills me with a certain amount of dread. I'd hate to mess it up.

PAUSE 3 seconds

Speaker Four

PAUSE 2 seconds

I wasn't exactly looking forward to it, as I was expecting her to be very negative about my performance in recent times. I'd anticipated what she might have a go at me for, and I'd prepared my defence. And indeed, she did start off by asking me how I thought I'd been doing recently, but I was surprised to see that she was very much on my side. It was, I thought, a very good piece of management, acknowledging that there was room for improvement but balancing it with praise for the positives.

PAUSE 3 seconds

Speaker Five

PAUSE 2 seconds

I thought there would be lots of arguments and very little would be agreed, if anything, because those people simply do not get on well together and don't have any respect for each other normally. Well, that's not what happened, this time everything went through smoothly and the whole thing was over in next to no time. Quite why it all went so well is something I can't work out. It doesn't make sense that they should suddenly all agree. There must be some logical reason but I can't see it.

PAUSE 10 seconds

Now you will hear Part 4 again.

TONE

REPEAT PART 4

PAUSE 5 seconds

That's the end of Part 4. There will now be a pause of five minutes for you to copy your answers onto the separate answer sheet. Be sure to follow the numbering of all the questions. Then your supervisor will collect all the question papers and answer sheets.

TEST 3

Cambridge Certificate of Proficiency in English Listening Test. Test 3. I'm going to give you the instructions for this test. I'll introduce each part of the test and give you time to look at the questions. At the start of each piece you'll hear this sound:

TONE

You'll hear each piece twice. Remember, while you're listening, write your answers on the question paper. You'll have five minutes at the end of the test to copy your answers onto the separate answer sheet. There will now be a pause. Please ask any questions now, because you must not speak during the test.

PAUSE 5 seconds

Now open your question paper and look at Part 1.

PAUSE 5 seconds

(PART ONE)

You will hear three different extracts. For questions **1–6**, choose the answer (**A**, **B** or **C**) which fits best according to what you hear. There are two questions for each extract.

Extract One

PAUSE 15 seconds

TONE

Female student: The first few weeks were a whirl and all the volunteers felt like they were on 'experience overload'. It is hard to convey the massive mental and physical adjustments you make when living in a developing country if all you have known is wall-to-wall Western comforts. As volunteers, we were encouraged to live at 'grass-root' level throughout the year – indeed, it was impossible not to on the meagre amount of pocket money we were allotted. This meant embracing the culture of the Transkei with open arms – whether you liked it or not. The traditional diet of meal, soup and home-made beer was not to be sampled but lived off, and I could forget any vegetarian tendencies I had because nobody misses out on their inyama, meat. I have learned much from the Transkei, not only about people's attitudes and ways of life but also about myself – by coping with difficult situations, experiencing successes and failures in the project, and doing it alone, miles away from my family.

PAUSE 5 seconds

TONE

REPEAT Extract One

PAUSE 2 seconds

Extract Two

PAUSE 15 seconds

TONE

Male actor: We specialize in participatory theatre. I'm interacting with the kids. You get a lot of feedback from them and they generate a lot of energy. Children are not guarded or non-committal in their response. In parks and

on adventure playgrounds they will leave if they don't like what you are doing. We find that we need to use different tactics for dealing with each situation. For instance, on adventure playgrounds we perform on high ground away from the play equipment to gain our audience. In schools, where children can be controlled, we have to work harder to get a response but we do get it. Response is essential to the progression of the entertainment. We have to be in control without resorting to repression. Disrupters usually have a reason for making a noise, so we try to take notice of them and act on their suggestions. We rarely say 'no'. At the end of the performance, we 'unmask'. This is part of the process of bringing the kids down again and it is very important. You can only responsibly involve kids in uninhibited action if you can bring about a return to 'normality' at the end.

PAUSE 5 seconds

TONE

REPEAT Extract Two

Pause 2 seconds

Extract Three

PAUSE 15 seconds

TONE

Man: Years ago, in a suburb far away, I could see my friend John whenever I wanted to. If I wanted to see John – and I always did, because we had such a laugh – I just knocked on his door and his mum would let me in. But when boys become men, the nature of friendship changes. When you're a boy, friends are a permanent presence in your life. They are ally, companion and support network. Perhaps it is only when we are boys, unencumbered by all the baggage of adult lives – careers, family and exhaustion – that we truly understand the nature of friendship. Now friends – even friends I love like brothers – are more distant figures. These friends – even the ones that will be there forever – are on the margins of my life, just as I am on the margins of their lives. Our meetings have to be meticulously scheduled because time is so scarce. And while I do understand the need for that formality, sometimes it seems like a negation of friendship. And sometimes I miss the years when I didn't have to look into my diary to work out when I could see my friends. Now and again I miss the intensity of the friendships we had as boys. And I miss my mate John.

PAUSE 5 seconds

TONE

REPEAT Extract Three

PAUSE 2 seconds

That's the end of Part 1. Now turn to Part 2.

PAUSE 5 seconds

(PART TWO)

You will hear part of a radio programme about the arts. For questions **7–15**, complete the sentences with a word or short phrase. You now have forty-five seconds in which to look at Part 2.

[PAUSE THE RECORDING FOR 45 SECONDS]
TONE

Presenter: Home may be a place of privacy and escape, but for some it is becoming less of a retreat and more of a place which people who come up with new jargon might term 'a multi-use environment'. And now we have the scenario of the home being thrown open to the public as an art gallery or cinema or virtually anything one chooses really, as long as it is fun or edifying. To tell me about some examples of this, I'm joined by our arts correspondent, Jasmine Wright. Jasmine, it all sounds a bit strange to me.

Jasmine: Well, it can be financially rewarding, though letting strangers into your home does require nerve. For example, there's a guy called Johnny Morris, he's an artist and designer who lives in east London, and he's decided to open his home under the title 'Gallery Ezra' to sell his and his friends' prints. He put a sign outside, opened the door and attracted some of the Sunday morning pedestrians that seethe along the flower market on his doorstep.

Presenter: Sounds a bit risky.

Jasmine: Yes, he told me that allowing the public into his home was not without its fraught aspects. He found it exhausting getting up early on a Sunday and having people walking around his flat with shopping bags. But he said that people were very well behaved and incredibly polite. His flatmate was less keen, apparently, and said he should have a rent reduction. But Johnny says that the venture was good for neighbourly relations and that it was such a financial success that he's going to open up again in spring.

Presenter: Well, good luck to him. Now, who else is doing it?

Jasmine: There's a couple, also in east London, Phoebe Tate and Gareth Harris, who've also opened a gallery in their house. It's called 'Made to Measure', named after the previous tenants who were tailors, and it consists of a small room at the front of the house which they're using as dedicated exhibition space. They say they don't want a gallery as such. According to Phoebe, who used to be an art consultant, it's important that it's part of the house, because their plan is, and I quote, 'to make art more domestic'. She says that nowadays a lot of art is monumentally sized and made for museums, but that throughout history it has been made for homes.

Presenter: Interesting idea. Do they get a lot of visitors?

Jasmine: Yes, the building itself is part of the attraction and a lot of their visitors are fascinated by the house. They've had to put up 'private' signs telling visitors where they cannot go. And while they stress that entrance is by appointment only, passers-by may come in if it's convenient.

Presenter: Worth a visit, in your view?

Jasmine: Definitely. And they also use the exhibition room for talks. Gareth, who's a goldsmith and a guide at the Victoria and Albert Museum, delivers historic accounts of the area from time to time, which I understand are well worth hearing.

Presenter: Now is this a 'London thing' and is it always about art?

Jasmine: No, and no. The sharing of a fantasy world may also be part of the open-house tendency. For example, well outside London, there's a couple, Norman and Valerie Illingworth, who've got a cinema in their garage, where invited guests can sit in genuine velvet cinema seats and watch a motorized curtain unfurl onto a programme of archive film material that includes cartoons, newsreels and adverts.

Presenter: What a terrific idea! Tell me more.

Jasmine: Well, Norman, who's 74, wears evening dress and Valerie, who's 56, acts as usherette, serving popcorn and ice-cream during the screenings. The creation of the atmosphere is the main point for them, with many authentic effects, including a 35mm projector housed in the former coal cellar. The Illingworths, who both used to work in the cinema and retained a permanent interest, are simply pleased to be able to share their enthusiasm in the comfort of their own garage. The garage is known as 'The Picturedome' and it's acquired a certain amount of local fame, despite the fact that screenings are not that frequent.

Presenter: Fascinating. Well, thanks Jasmine. So, if you'd like to open your house up for ...

PAUSE 10 seconds
Now you'll hear Part 2 again.
TONE
REPEAT Part 2
PAUSE 5 seconds
That's the end of Part 2. Now turn to Part 3.
PAUSE 5 seconds

(PART THREE)

You will hear an interview with a sports writer about football referees. For questions **16–20**, choose the answer (**A, B, C** or **D**) which fits best according to what you hear. You now have one minute in which to look at Part 3.
[PAUSE THE RECORDING FOR 1 MINUTE]
TONE

Presenter: I'm talking to Martin Groves, who's written a series of articles about football referees. Martin, something you discovered, didn't you, that most people might not realize, is how competitive the average referee is?

Martin: Yes, referees regard selection for the most glamorous matches, such as cup finals and international games, with every bit as much longing and pride as players do. They suffer from tension before and during matches. They admit to jealousy and vindictiveness among their fraternity. They become minor celebrities. They receive letters of praise and sour abuse from people they have never met. They see themselves as part of the action, closer to it than managers and coaches. Just as with the players, it is when a referee stops getting letters and is no longer being booed outside football grounds that he worries most about his future.

Presenter: What's the relationship between players and referees really like then, Martin?

Martin: Referees like to feel that they are respected by players for their astuteness and their fairness. They are, in this respect, like schoolteachers who regard themselves as close to the boys, or police detectives who think that give-and-take with criminals is the best way to deal with them in the long run. For example, I spoke to one referee who expressed this attitude explicitly when he said, with evident pleasure and pride, that a certain international player, known for his unpredictable temper, 'responds to the right treatment'. By and large, he found professional footballers were 'a great crowd', which is generous of him, considering the low opinion players are often prepared to give of referees. It's striking how closely referees like to align themselves with the players, in contrast with the scorn with which players will detach themselves from connection with referees. There is no question about who would like to change places with whom.

Presenter: Now what makes someone want to be a referee?

Martin: It is a romantic and, it seems to me, most unrealistic view of refereeing to say, as one president of the international football authority FIFA once did, that 'it is a job for volunteers, who are doing a service to their country'. Plainly it is not public-spiritedness that motivates men into the ambition of controlling big football matches, even if the authorities insist on treating them like servants of duty. As with managers and directors, there is undoubtedly a deep absorption in football here, and the material reward is insubstantial to say the least. But there is much more satisfying of ego than disinterest in the motive. The referee wants to be recognized in the game, and he wants to feel he is important to it. He even wants to be liked.

Presenter: Now referees get assessed, don't they, they get given marks for their performance in each game by representatives of the clubs involved, don't they?

Martin: Yes, and the reports on the referee are sent to the football authorities, to whom the referees are directly responsible. So the referee is in the unsatisfactory position of a consultant brought in to adjudicate, instructed to brook no interference and then made subject to the criticism of his employers on the grounds that he was not up to the job. Under these circumstances one referee I spoke to could hardly be said to be overstating the referee's predicament when he said that he needed, above all else, 'a skin like a rhinoceros and to be as deaf as a post'. Fire is breathed on him from the crowd, obscenity may be muttered at him by the players and afterwards he can be accused of both laxity and over-zealousness by assessors. As that referee said: 'The referee's only got to make one bad mistake and

everything else he does in the game is forgotten.'

Presenter: So they're under a lot of pressure. I mean, referees get some awful stick from players, don't they? That must put them off quite a bit.

Martin: Yes, but a referee ought to be able to differentiate quickly between the spontaneous expletives of angered players and the malevolent abuse of those trying to intimidate him. In a game which creates as much passion and as much demand on a man's resources as does professional football, there are bound to be moments when gamesmanship and outright villainy test a referee to his limit. There are also times when he has to decide instantly which of the two is present in an incident. The good referee is not the man who plays safe with either a blind eye or a public display of moral outrage, but the one who can unobtrusively deal with the offence and defuse the situation.

Presenter: Who'd be a referee? Thanks, Martin. And now, ...

PAUSE 10 seconds

Now you'll hear Part 3 again.

TONE

REPEAT Part 3

PAUSE 5 seconds

That's the end of Part 3. Now turn to Part 4.

PAUSE 5 seconds

(PART FOUR)

Part 4 consists of two tasks. You will hear five short extracts in which people are talking about something currently in the news. Look at Task 1. For questions **21–25**, choose from the list (**A–H**) what the news story concerns. Now look at Task 2. For questions **26–30**, choose from the list (**A–H**) each speaker's attitude towards the news story. While you listen, you must complete both tasks. You now have forty-five seconds in which to look at Part 4.

[PAUSE THE RECORDING FOR 45 SECONDS]

TONE

Speaker One

PAUSE 2 seconds

I don't know, you read these things all the time, and if you took them all to heart you wouldn't do anything! And they seem to contradict each other all the time too. One time you're told that you should do this and that and then you get told that it's wrong to do it and it'll have bad consequences for you. This one is particularly scary because it says that something most people do is potentially harmful. Frankly, I find it hard to take it seriously, and I'm inclined to doubt that it's true, whatever they say.

PAUSE 3 seconds

Speaker Two

PAUSE 2 seconds

I know a lot of people have become cynical about all this, and for good reason, but I genuinely feel that this could represent something very good for the future. Finally, someone has come along who's saying all the right things as far as I'm concerned and I can't see any downside to that. We need people in charge who aren't just out for themselves, who genuinely want to do good for the majority. And I think that's exactly what she is so I'm glad she looks like she's having a good chance of taking over the leadership.

PAUSE 3 seconds

Speaker Three

PAUSE 2 seconds

I don't see way anyone takes this sort of thing seriously. Here we have someone who's somehow managed to rise to the top, presumably with the aid of publicists and the like, in something that's really quite trivial. They get all the wealth and all the attention and it goes to their heads, so some of them start to think their opinions are incredibly important. It really irritates me – why would I want to hear what he thinks of what's going on in the country and the world? He talks adolescent rubbish and it infuriates me that he gets indulged in this, as if he matters.

PAUSE 3 seconds

Speaker Four

PAUSE 2 seconds

When this kind of thing happens, and it's all over the media for a while, it gets everyone worked up and they start to think it could happen to them. But of course, such incidents are very rare and that's why they're in the papers and on TV. Horrible as it is, and I feel very sorry for the victims, it doesn't mean that we have to fear that this sort of thing is likely to happen all the time. I don't let this kind of thing get to me, you just have to carry on regardless.

PAUSE 3 seconds

Speaker Five

PAUSE 2 seconds

You often read or see these things that claim to be about how people live these days, about what's going on in general, some new trend, and they make all these questionable assumptions. Usually, what they're actually doing is talking about how they live, what's going on around them, and they're a privileged minority. The rest of us couldn't possibly afford to have that kind of lifestyle, and therefore we don't have the sort of problems they talk about. So I just ignore what they're saying because it has no relevance at all to me or anyone I know.

PAUSE 10 seconds

Now you will hear Part 4 again.

TONE

REPEAT PART 4

PAUSE 5 seconds

That's the end of Part 4. There will now be a pause of five minutes for you to copy your answers onto the separate answer sheet. Be sure to follow the numbering of all the questions. Then your supervisor will collect all the question papers and answer sheets.

TEST 4

Cambridge Certificate of Proficiency in English Listening Test. Test 4.

I'm going to give you the instructions for this test. I'll introduce each part of the test and give you time to look at the questions. At the start of each piece you'll hear this sound:

TONE

You'll hear each piece twice.

Remember, while you're listening, write your answers on the question paper. You'll have five minutes at the end of the test to copy your answers onto the separate answer sheet. There will now be a pause. Please ask any questions now, because you must not speak during the test.

PAUSE 5 seconds

Now open your question paper and look at Part 1.

PAUSE 5 seconds

(PART ONE)

You will hear three different extracts. For questions **1–6**, choose the answer (**A**, **B** or **C**) which fits best according to what you hear. There are two questions for each extract.

Extract One

PAUSE 15 seconds

TONE

Woman: They have been around for about 350 million years. They are very beautiful, even though they spend years under water as space monster lookalikes. They can fly across continents and oceans, yet they are in danger of becoming extinct. The National Dragonfly Museum, with its team of volunteer wildlife helpers, is dedicated to ensuring that the dragonfly survives and thrives. As the guiding spirit and chairman of the Museum puts it in the brochure: 'They have been around 350 times longer than we have and now, because of us and our pollution, dragonflies are having a hard time. But let's not sit back clutching our eco-guilt. There are things we can do.'
As many as 200 dragonfly-spotters turn up on any open day during the summer. But there's no telling which species will show up from one day to the next, it all depends on the weather. Dragonflies refuse to fly in overcast conditions. They sulk. Nevertheless, dragonfly action can go on with lectures, exhibitions and videos throughout the day. Fans of the horror film *Alien* can treat themselves to a frisson of recognition by watching a wide-screen projection of dragonfly larvae snatching and devouring prey. Not a spectacle for the squeamish.

PAUSE 5 seconds

TONE

REPEAT Extract One

PAUSE 2 seconds

Extract Two

PAUSE 15 seconds
TONE
Presenter: Richie Stachowski is still in his teens but already he has made his fortune – several million dollars, earned with the sort of entrepreneurial brainwave that commands respect, as well as envy. He had an idea for a novel swimming-pool toy, a walkie-talkie he called the 'Water Talkie'. It was an instant hit. There is no doubt that the Water Talkie was Richie's idea, and grown-up toy makers testify that he has a gift for new ideas. The concept just popped into his head, he says, while he was snorkelling with his Dad in the sea off Hawaii.
Richie: I saw all this amazing stuff down there, and I really wanted to talk about it with my Dad while we were swimming along. And then I thought: 'Hey! Why don't we invent something so that we can talk under water?'
Presenter: The snag, he thought, was that all the wires and batteries of a walkie-talkie would get wet.
Richie: My granddad was a big navy guy and he was on submarines or something, so my Dad said he might know how to do it. He put us on to sonar underwater acoustics. I was really surprised to learn that sound works better under water.
Presenter: Richie went on to have a hand in making sure the toy 'looked nice' and the Water Talkie was promptly sold to some of the world's biggest toy retailers.
PAUSE 5 seconds
TONE
REPEAT Extract Two
PAUSE 2 seconds
Extract Three
PAUSE 15 seconds
TONE
Female author: You could argue that there are similarities between fiction and cookbook writing. My own book certainly attempts to be a work of evocation. But in a sense this is the case even with more picture-led and less word-driven enterprises, too. Just as in the novel, what is attempted is the portrayal of a life, a world, a series of values, aspirations, emotions. You might also say that this world that is evoked, this series of values, is indeed, and most emphatically a fiction. For it is hardly difficult to notice that there is something of a disparity between cookbook culture – real food, lovingly created, lingeringly appreciated – and real life. To be frank, this disparity alone would be enough to explain the cookbook obsession. We no longer, really, lead domestic lives. We are work creatures, we live in offices. Naturally, then, our desires turn to the home. That is why there is such a proliferation of writing on cooking and interior decoration. Words have to make up for the shortfall in deeds. Don't be fooled by cookbook consumption: reading about food is what you do instead of cooking it. We are talking vicarious gratification here.

PAUSE 5 seconds
TONE
REPEAT Extract Three
PAUSE 2 seconds
That's the end of Part 1. Now turn to Part 2.
PAUSE 5 seconds

(PART TWO)
You will hear part of a talk about shopping centres. For questions 7–15, complete the sentences with a word or short phrase. You now have forty-five seconds in which to look at Part 2.
[PAUSE THE RECORDING FOR 45 SECONDS]
TONE
David Peek: My name, as you probably know, is David Peek. I act as a consultant to the developers of shopping centres, advising their architects pand designers on what makes customers switch their loyalties from an existing store and travel sometimes relatively long distances to a new one. It's rather a fancy term, but I'm what is known as a 'consumer behaviourist'. Now, there are two fundamental questions when it comes to building a shopping centre. First, is the money there, and second, how do we get it, as opposed to somebody else? The answer is to make people feel comfortable and enthusiastic about the proposition. Increasingly, as shoppers become more discerning and competition increases, this means focusing on things such as safety, air quality, light and choice of materials – what I call 'total sensory design' – as well as perennially important things such as value and service. I've identified 12 key stages the shopper goes through from leaving the comfort of the couch to returning home, which need to be 'de-stressed'. I begin my work miles away from the site, since research indicates that problems getting to a shopping centre make people regard the whole experience as negative. Too many roundabouts on the drive there are, I've found, stressful for women. They also don't like litter in the surrounding areas. Research has also indicated that people want 25 per cent more space round their cars in the car park to manoeuvre push-chairs and trolleys. In terms of the materials used within a shopping centre, the flooring materials are especially important. Shiny surfaces are out, because they can be slippery and make people afraid of falling. I've found that people inevitably gravitate towards natural materials. They may admire plastic and steel for their design qualities, but they develop relationships with stone and wood. They're much more expensive, but I'm convinced that they make people think of a location with them as superior. Now what if people just feel that a place is not for them? What if the pensioners hate the designer clothes and loud music designed for people in their 20s? Well, I've thought of this problem, of course. In my view, people like to shop

with like-minded people, what I call 'People Like Us', or PLUs for short. So in the latest shopping centre I've been involved with, shops are grouped in what I refer to as 'PLU clusters', so that people likely to be drawn to one sort of shop will not feel threatened by people drawn to another. Thus, the centre has the exclusive mall and the discount mall and shoppers visiting one of them need never meet shoppers going to the other. My research has identified six consumer 'types'. For example, there are those who respond to understated presentation which enables them to pride themselves on their shrewdness; these I call 'County Classics'. Pensioners and people who have stopped competing in their careers fall into another category – 'Home Comfortables'. Then there are people who look out for some code which tells them a place is for them and not for others; I call them 'Club Executives'. They want comfort and value, not aesthetics. Another category covers people who don't have huge spending power but always think they're going to find a bargain – the 'Budget Optimists'. Then there are what I call 'Young Fashionables', who lack analytical skills but know what they want when they see it and go for it voraciously. And finally, there are couples, just married, with one income and just about getting by, who I call 'Young Survivors'. People sometimes ask me if I ever feel guilty about making people spend money they don't want to spend. What I say is that I have a strong aversion to conning people. I believe that to earn money in the retail business, you must give outstanding value. Now that brings me on to my next point, which concerns ...

PAUSE 10 seconds
Now you'll hear Part 2 again.
TONE
REPEAT Part 2
PAUSE 5 seconds
That's the end of Part 2. Now turn to Part 3.
PAUSE 5 seconds

(PART THREE)

You will hear part of a radio programme about journalists who interview famous people. For questions **16–20**, choose the answer (**A**, **B**, **C** or **D**) which fits best according to what you hear. You now have one minute in which to look at Part 3.

[PAUSE THE RECORDING FOR 1 MINUTE]
TONE

Presenter: Journalism has become a subject for serious study, judging by the number of schools and colleges offering courses and degrees in media studies. Students now write theses on the Art of Interviewing. We are in something of a mini golden age for the Celebrity Interview. Just open any British paper or magazine. In Britain, almost every paper has its star interviewer. The bylines are big, the space generous and the remuneration handsome. Rival papers try to lure away star interviewers, the way they once fought over the Big Columnist or the Voice of Sport, knowing that a good interview, with a good name, sells papers. But who are these interviewers and how do they do it? I spoke first to Lynn Barber, who's been interviewing famous people, or FPs, for many years for a variety of national newspapers.

Lynn Barber: Left to myself, I tend to choose interviewees who are male, older than myself and difficult. I don't mind if they are vain, egotistical or badly behaved. I avoid nice, sane, straightforward people. My best subjects are the last people on earth you would want to meet at a dinner party. I usually start with a clever, complicated question like 'You said in one paper in 1996 blah blah blah, whereas you told a magazine in 1998 blah blah blah.' This is to let them see that I've done my homework, that I've made an effort and so should they, and that I won't be fobbed off with old answers. Then I might go on to some soft questions about childhood, finishing with a few more provocative observations, carefully worded, such as 'It seems to me you are very arrogant', just to get them going.

Presenter: For Zoe Heller, each interview is a week's work.

Zoe Heller: It does look like a breeze, interviewing one person and taking a week over it. I've got faster, but I still write very slowly. I don't know how people manage without a tape recorder. I couldn't do it. You couldn't possibly get their exact words. I often send them one of my previous pieces in advance, showing them what they're in for, what they can expect. If they agree to see me, I expect them to play the game. There always is a dilemma. I fret about upsetting people but at the same time I want to describe them honestly. Quite a few people have been upset. I wouldn't be interviewed by me. Or by anyone. God, no. I spend a whole week persuading someone to do something that I wouldn't do myself in a month of Sundays.

Presenter: Angela Lambert, a very experienced interviewer, doesn't use a tape recorder, she makes notes in longhand during the interview.

Angela Lambert: When I arrive, I usually explain that everything that happens belongs to me, though if they say something is off the record, I won't write it down. If they are nervous, I'll say, 'Look, trust me, otherwise you won't enjoy it and I won't enjoy it. If you're really nervous, I'll abandon it.' I have no hidden agenda. If of course they behave badly, and are beastly, I'll write that down. At the end, I say if they have any regrets, then say it now. They hardly ever take anything back, except trivial things, such as perhaps 'Don't mention my brother'. A great many interviewees mistake intimacy for real friendship. There is reciprocal warmth, which can be very embarrassing, as I'm highly unlikely to see them again. If you are doing an ordinary human interest story, I know that my sympathy will stop the moment the interview is over. They don't realize that, but I feel guilty. If it's a so-called celebrity interview, then that doesn't matter. I don't feel guilty. They know the ropes.

Presenter: Ray Connolly is one of the few male journalists rated by the women in the field.

Ray Connolly: As for my approach, I try to tell a story, with a beginning, a middle and an end, in order to make it readable. That's why chat-show interviews are so poor. The best bit might be in the first minute, or the last minute. With a written interview, you can shape it to get the best effect. If asked, I will let people see the interview, but I don't offer. In 30 years, I've had few complaints. I often protect people from themselves. They don't realize what they say, how things might hurt their children. I like doing writers best. I like actors least. They have nothing to say.

Presenter: Now, as an interviewer myself, this got me thinking …

PAUSE 10 seconds

Now you'll hear Part 3 again.

TONE

REPEAT Part Three

PAUSE 5 seconds

That's the end of Part Three. Now turn to Part Four.

PAUSE 5 seconds

(PART FOUR)

Part 4 consists of two tasks. You will hear five short extracts in which people are talking about people they know. Look at Task 1. For questions **21–25**, choose from the list (**A–H**) what each speaker says is a good characteristic of the person. Now look at Task 2. For questions **26–30**, choose from the list (**A–H**) what each speaker regards as a bad characteristic of the person. While you listen, you must complete both tasks. You now have forty-five seconds in which to look at Part 4.

[PAUSE THE RECORDING FOR 45 SECONDS]

TONE

Speaker One

PAUSE 2 seconds

James is someone who stands by his friends – once you're a friend of his, you're always a friend of his. It doesn't matter what you do, or what other people say about you, he's a friend for life. We've had our ups and downs over the years, but that's one of the things I really like about him. Strangely enough, though, he has a completely different side to him, and he often comes out with things I would regard as offensive and personally insulting. He's not exactly what you'd call tactful – he just comes right out and says what's on his mind.

PAUSE 3 seconds

Speaker Two

PAUSE 2 seconds

Nothing fazes Alex, whatever happens she just takes it in her stride and gets on with life, which is what I really admire about her. She's been through all sorts of changes and problems, but she's always managed to do whatever

she has to do in the circumstances. She doesn't expect things to go her way or stay the same all the time. There are lots of issues I don't discuss with her though. She's got her own very fixed opinions and she simply won't listen to any alternative point of view.

PAUSE 3 seconds

Speaker Three

PAUSE 2 seconds

What people don't necessarily notice about Tammy is how sharp she is. She doesn't miss anything, and she can see right through people. When everyone else is talking about something that's happened, she gets straight to the heart of the matter. She's hardly ever wrong, either. Of course, most people she knows don't realise this because she isn't very talkative and she generally lets other people lead the conversation. If she was more outgoing, didn't hold back so much, people would have a much higher opinion of her.

PAUSE 3 seconds

Speaker Four

PAUSE 2 seconds

I know that some people laugh at Jessie and think she's a bit of a fool and, well, she does come out with some outrageous things and make some very public mistakes. But the great thing about her is she never lets any of that get to her, she just carries on believing in herself, never doubting for a minute that what she's doing is the right thing. What I don't like so much, though, is her tendency to have tantrums when things don't go her way – that kind of behaviour is just plain embarrassing for someone of her age.

PAUSE 3 seconds

Speaker Five

PAUSE 2 seconds

Chris is one of those people who never gives up – if he wants to do something, he carries on however badly things are going or whatever setbacks he has. I think that's a great strength of his, he never knows when he's beaten. One problem though is that he thinks everyone else should do the same, and he never makes allowances for other people's weaknesses. Because he thinks life is tough and you have to be hard, he has no time for people who complain about their problems.

PAUSE 10 seconds

Now you will hear Part 4 again.

TONE

REPEAT PART 4

PAUSE 5 seconds

That's the end of Part 4. There will now be a pause of five minutes for you to copy your answers onto the separate answer sheet. Be sure to follow the numbering of all the questions. Then your supervisor will collect all the question papers and answer sheets.